WATERLINE WARSHIPS

WATERLINE WARSHIPS

An Illustrated Masterclass

PHILIP REED

Seaforth
PUBLISHING

Copyright © Philip Reed 2010

First published in Great Britain in 2010 by
Seaforth Publishing,
Pen & Sword Books Ltd,
47 Church Street,
Barnsley S70 2AS

www.seaforthpublishing.com

British Library Cataloguing in Publication Data
A catalogue record for this book is available from the British Library

ISBN 978 1 84832 076 5

Typeset and designed by Ian Hughes
Printed and bound in China

▪ Contents ▪

▪ Introduction ▪

Although the majority of my work has been in the field of the sailing ship, I have over the years built sixteen modern warship models, mainly focussing on the two World Wars. They have always been interesting and involving subjects and I am sure I would have built many more had not a succession of commissions taken me in other directions. My fascination with the warships of this era was almost certainly engendered by childhood visits to the Imperial War Museum, particularly the Norman Ough models which, over the years, I came to revere.

Early in my modelmaking life when I had, I think, three large-scale sailing ship models under my belt, I decided I wanted to try my hand at a twentieth-century warship, and being particularly fond of Norman Ough's model of the cruiser HMS *Curacao*, ordered a set of his plans for her. These were the first modern warship plans I had ever examined and I was initially rather confused by the complexity of these vessels, everything being so new to me, and I felt doubtful as to whether I would ever be able to make sense of them, let alone build a model from them. Time and further examination confirmed this opinion and they were consigned to the plans drawer; no model of *Curacao* was ever built.

I next made a brief excursion into the world of the plastic kit, gaining a little knowledge and experience, but kits were rather limited in those days and I had none of the information on detailing or painting that is readily available today, let alone the then unheard-of extras like brass etch. One kit model I was happy with was of HMS *Belfast*, to which I added a 'Flower' class corvette, HMS *Bluebell*. I managed numerous 'improvements' to the *Belfast* and built the corvette myself, so opening the door to the scratch-building world. These two models were, however, built to a scale of 50ft to 1in and the museum models I so wished to emulate were mostly built to the scale of 16ft to 1in. I now feel that this scale is about the ideal for ship models of smaller vessels but impractical for a large cruiser or battleship where 32ft to 1in is more appropriate, certainly for the average domestic setting; you will find this reflected in the Model Gallery at the end of the book. But I should add that this is only my personal opinion and other modellers will have their favoured scales.

After completing the *Belfast* diorama, and still determined to build a larger-scale model, I purchased a set of Norman Ough's plans for the 'Tribal' class destroyer HMS *Matabele* from which I planned to build a model of her sister-ship *Cossack*, and, as with the models of *Belfast* and *Bluebell*, details of these early and rather basic models are provided in the Model Gallery, and these should lend hope to the aspiring scratch-builder.

With *Cossack* finished there was no holding me, and there followed a succession of models. To begin with, they were almost all built to 32ft to 1in. Then sailing ship work began to dominate my time, leaving little time for forays into the twentieth century. So, being asked recently to build a Second World War destroyer I was not only delighted to undertake the commission but also saw it as an ideal opportunity to write a book outlining the project and describing the techniques.

HMS *Dido* 1940
Scale 16' to 1''

7

My client and I eventually – and after much discussion over configuration and camouflage – settled on the War Emergency destroyer HMS *Caesar*. She carried a camouflage scheme that we both found attractive and I had reliable information for the colours used and, last but not least, there was a set of plans for her at 16ft to 1in along with large-scale plans for virtually all armament and fittings available from John Lambert Plans.

With all this information you might anticipate plain sailing, but if you have any experience of modelmaking you will know differently; almost from the word go, queries and doubts will arise about just about everything. The modeller needs to accumulate all the photographic and other reference material that he can to back up the plans. Ideally, evidence should consist of onboard photographs of the prototype or a sister-ship. Photographs of an accurate museum-quality model are also helpful (though always remember to be sceptical and check for accuracy), and if it is possible to take the photographs yourself, from every angle, all the better. With *Caesar*, however, this was not an option. I failed to locate a model of a 'Ca.' or any other of the War Emergency class destroyers, and the only good on-board photos are, I believe held by the National Archives of Scotland who own the John Brown collection of negatives. At the time these had been withdrawn while the collection was re-catalogued. Fortunately, most or all of these are reproduced in *Warship Profile No. 32 H.M.S. Cavalier and the Ca. Class Destroyers* by Anthony Preston. I assembled files on the 'C' class in general as well as others for camouflage, bridge, funnel, mast, 4.5in guns, Hazemeyer Bofors, Oerlikons, boats, davits, depth-charge gear, torpedo tubes, searchlights, vents and lockers, sights and sea. I also took photographs of all the large-scale plans and drawings I had for any of the above and added these to the relevant files. This allows quick access when I want to consult them for any detail of construction, though it is worth emphasising that I always start from the original plans when taking meas-urements or preparing a tracing.

I then visited HMS *Cavalier*, *Caesar*'s sister-ship, preserved at Chatham Historic Dockyard, and took many photos of her, though it was more of a pilgrimage than an information-gathering trip as so much of the original ship has disappeared in successive refits. However, it gave me a sense of scale and a real feel of being on one of these ships, something I believe is a very valuable addition to the research armoury.

Above all, building any model should be a fulfilling and pleasurable undertaking, though by its nature not without problems and difficulties and probably a few major frustrations and even disasters, but it is in the overcoming of these and finally bringing the project to fruition that the real rewards are to be found. Which reminds me of a favourite and very apt quote by Thomas Harris, author of *The Silence of the Lambs*: 'Problem solving is hunting, it is savage pleasure and we are born to it.' Happy hunting.

PHILIP REED

▪ The Ship: HMS *Caesar* 1944 ▪

The 'Ca.' class War Emergency Destroyers

The eight 'Ca.' ships were the first group of the thirty-two 'C' class destroyers built between 1943 and 1945, forming the 11th Emergency Flotilla. They were based on the pre-war 'J' class destroyers, somewhat simplified to facilitate rapid mass-production in wartime. They were armed with the 4.5in gun that had been introduced in the previous 'Z' class, and retained a powerful torpedo battery to defend convoys against surface raiders. The class saw some wartime service, but by 1953 they were obsolete and so all eight were taken in hand for extensive modernisation, the last re-entering service in 1961. The ships were fitted with modern fire-control apparatus, radars and sonars. 'X' gun and the after set of torpedo tubes were removed and replaced with a pair of Squid three-barrelled anti-submarine mortars. The anti-aircraft armament was changed to a twin 40mm Mk 5 Bofors mount aft and two single Bofors either side of the bridge. This upgrade, the most extensive applied to any wartime-built destroyers apart from those converted to frigates, greatly enhanced their capabilities as general-purpose escorts and the last of them was not stricken from service until 1972.

The 'Ca.' class as built

Displacement:	1,710 tons standard; 2,530 tons full load
Dimensions:	
length	339.3ft pp; 350ft wl; 362.75ft oa
beam	35.75ft
draught (max)	14.25ft
Machinery:	2 x Admiralty 3-drum boilers; Parsons single reduction geared turbines; 40,000 SHP = 36 knots. Range = 4,675 miles @ 20 knots
Armament:	4 x 4.5in guns (4 x 1); 2 x 40mm Bofors (1 x 2); 6 x 20mm Oerlikon (2 x 2; 2 x 1); 8 x 21in torpedo tubes (2 x 4); 2 x depth-charge racks, 4 x depth-charge throwers
Crew:	186
Ships in class:	*Caesar, Cavendish, Cambrian, Carron, Caprice, Cassandra, Carysfort, Cavalier*

HMS *Caesar*

HMS *Caesar*, the sixth ship of her class, was built by John Brown of Clydebank. Laid down on 3 April 1943, she was launched on 14 February 1944 and completed on 5 October that year. She was fitted with extra accommodation for her role as a flotilla leader. She joined the Home Fleet in November 1944, and on the 14th of that month was part of the escort for the aircraft carrier HMS *Pursuer* when she launched air attacks on German shipping off Tromsø in Norway. In December she joined the escort of the Russian-bound Convoy JW62, arriving at the Kola inlet on the 7th and returning to Loch Ewe on the 19th with Convoy RA52. During this voyage *Caesar*'s sister-ship HMS *Cassandra* was torpedoed and badly damaged by *U-365*, which was itself sunk by aircraft from the escort carrier HMS *Nairana* two days later.

At the beginning of 1945 *Caesar* initially served with the Home Fleet, and was then transferred to the Atlantic for convoy defence in the Western Approaches. In April

HMS *Caesar*
(Courtesy
John Lambert)

1945 she was nominated for Far Eastern service and began a refit in preparation for joining the Eastern Fleet. However, in June 1945 she escorted the cruiser HMS *Jamaica* taking the King and Queen on a visit to the Channel Islands, and did not sail for Colombo until 15 July, arriving on 7 August. She returned to Plymouth and paid off on 28 May 1946. She was then held in reserve, undergoing a minor refit in 1955–6, before being taken in hand for the major modernisation her class received (see above) in November 1957, during which she was one of four ships to receive an enclosed frigate-style bridge. She returned to active service in late 1960, and in April 1961 she replaced her sister-ship HMS *Cavendish* as the leader of the 8th Destroyer Squadron in the Far East, where she experienced four gruelling years of patrol duty, including the confrontation with Indonesia. She returned to Portsmouth in 1965, and was placed on the disposal list. After being de-equipped at Chatham Dockyard, she was sold for scrap in 1966 and arrived at the breaker's yard in Blyth on 6 January 1967.

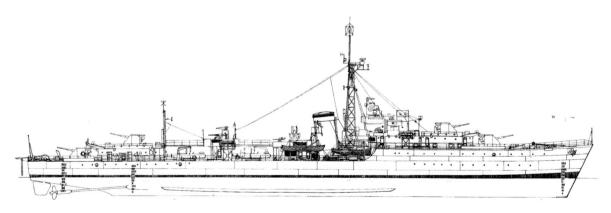

HMS *Caesar* (Courtesy John Lambert)

HMS *Cavalier*

HMS *Cavalier*

HMS *Caesar*'s sister-ship HMS *Cavalier* is the sole surviving British war-built destroyer. Launched on 28 February 1943 and completed on 22 November 1944, she was modernised in the 1950s along with the rest of her class, in her case retaining the original bridge. In 1966 *Cavalier* received a quadruple Seacat surface-to-air missile system, the launcher and handling room for it replacing the twin Bofors gun and the remaining set of torpedo tubes. She finally paid off in 1972, but after a campaign to preserve her lead by Lord Louis Mountbatten, she was purchased for £65,000 by the Cavalier Trust in 1977. She was displayed initially at Southampton and then for some years in Brighton, but in 1987 she was moved to Tyneside to be the centrepiece of a proposed shipbuilding museum. Unfortunately, this project came to nothing, and she was in danger of being scrapped. However, in 1998 she was bought by Chatham Historic Dockyard in Kent, where she is now on permanent display in dry-dock. On 14 November 2007 HMS *Cavalier* was officially designated a war memorial to the 142 Royal Navy destroyers sunk during the Second World War.

▪ The Workshop, Tools and Materials ▪

Before moving on to the model it seems appropriate to set the scene with a few words about the materials and tools I use. I now have a small but well-equipped workshop that provides virtually all the facilities that I need. It is, I must admit, in my later years a constant comfort and valued retreat, where I can withdraw from the world and immerse myself in my chosen subject far from everyday problems and stresses. This was not always so: when I was younger, much younger, married, and teaching for a living and then later, divorced and raising my two sons and building models professionally, modelmaking had to be fitted in whenever a little time could be found, most frequently on the living-room table and in the early days at least I had little access to machine tools. But I had energy and boundless enthusiasm and managed to build a variety of ship types to various scales with very basic resources; models ranging from a 1/32in to 1ft battleship to a 3/8in to 1ft sailing schooner. Timber was also an issue; I picked up whatever I could, wherever I found it. I once was given a 3-foot long log of sycamore by the gardener at the school where I was teaching at the time and spent many arduous lunch hours sawing it into 2in-square billets, some of which are still in my shed forty years later. Hand tools can be hard work and less accurate than their modern counterparts but using them certainly hones one's skills.

However, back to the present, and for those who might be interested, here are a few details of my rather self-indulgent workshop. Though having said that, if you bundled together the cost of the most useful of my machine tools and their fittings it may just amount to enough to keep an average smoker going for a year; so, just a question of priorities I suppose, and they have, of course, been acquired over many years.

The first requirement is obviously a space in which to work; nowadays this is mostly done at this fairly small area of bench which equates fairly well with the large wooden tray that I used to use on the living room

Plate A

Plate B

Plate C

table. **Plate A** shows my workbench in a decidedly cluttered and untidy state I'm afraid: if I had known it would be used for publication I would have tidied up a bit. The tray I used as an early work surface would be returned to a cupboard when work was finished for the evening. With a workshop, however, this is unnecessary and all the other facilities required are readily at hand. Now I don't have to reach far in any direction for the various materials I need for the vast majority of my work; they are stored in drawers and cupboards surrounding where I sit. The room is small, but adequate, and next door is an even smaller one, little more than a cupboard, where I normally use the machine tools, most of which are designed for the modelmaker so are correspondingly miniature. These comprise a jigsaw, Preac circular saw, Preac thicknesser, Unimat lathe and a grinder and polisher. They are all served by a very efficient home-made dust-extraction system powered by a domestic vacuum cleaner. I also have a dust extractor in the main workshop. This is housed in the loft space, the 2in hose feeding through the wall and connecting to a flexible hose that can be placed in any position over the workbench. This is invaluable when working with a rotary hand piece fitted with burrs or sanding disks; it can also be rigged with an extension hose to become a standard vacuum for the workshop, or, if I am using one of the power tools in the main workshop, the extension hose can be used to extract dust from this. The whole system is certainly somewhat Heath Robinson, but it ensures even with the amount of sawing and sanding etc. that I do the workshop is probably the most dust-free room in the house.

   Plate B features the computer and research area, in this instance, I have to admit, looking rather uncharacteristically tidy. I only have to spin around in my seat to access all necessary information, which in the case of *Caesar* became quite formidable. Digital storage is fast replacing my bulky old filing cabinets and I love it!

   When it comes to hand tools I am sure that any of you contemplating scratch-building a warship model will already have a selection of your own choosing. You will see the ones that I find most use for featuring in many of the illustrations. **Plate C** shows a selection of the more essential. From the left: dividers, nowadays an ordinary pair would be fine, but I, rather sadly, date from a time when the only feasible and affordable way to reduce or enlarge plans was using a pair of proportional dividers. They were then, and

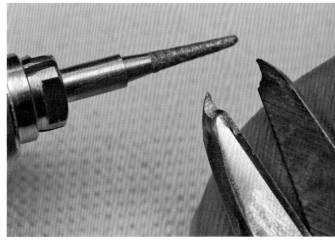

Plate D

Plate E

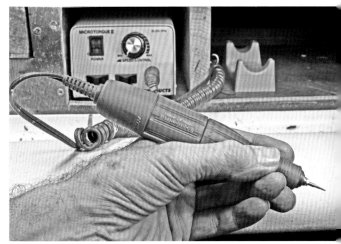

Plate F

presumably still are, prohibitively expensive, so unless you have a specific need don't go there.

Next are an absolute essential – several pairs of tweezers. Go to a supplier of jewellery or surgical goods and buy the best, not the best you can afford, but the best; you won't regret doing so. I basically use size No. 5, though they grow shorter with repeated sharpening and one old pair I have bent at the tip for those awkward situations. Tweezers do benefit from a little attention from time to time. If the tips get bent outwards as sometimes happens they should be realigned using a small pair of pliers, after which some fine emery paper can be drawn repeatedly between the ends while they are held closed. If the ends get broken or otherwise damaged they can be re-sharpened on a grind wheel or with a sanding disk in a rotary hand tool.

Sharp craft knives are another essential, I have always used Swan Morton scalpels with either a No. 10a or 11 blade. They are excellent for most of the work but I have come increasingly reliant on the red handled Swan Morton SM knives, I use their 01 craft blades shaped and sharpened on the TOMEK grind wheel. They take a razor-sharp edge and of course can be endlessly re-sharpened.

The scissors shown are one of three pairs I have. They were advertised as chrome hardened and suitable for cutting all materials including brass and copper. I have had them for years now and they are still showing no sign of blunting; their main use is for cutting wire rigging close to a spar or other part of a model after fitting. As I am sure you will have found out, normal scissors are not suited to this task. They just don't want to get close enough to the desired cutting point and don't work well at the extreme tip. To overcome this problem the ends of the scissors have been ground thinner on the grind wheel and semicircular scallops cut in the ends of both blades with a fine diamond burr, as shown in **Plate D**; the tips should be needle-sharp and should come together before the curved edge of the scallop.

Also shown in the picture are a small straight edge and a couple of useful squares. There are of course many other tools, far too many to list, that I have accumulated over the years, many of them only occasionally brought into use, but those shown above are the ones most frequently and essentially used.

Now a few words about power tools suited to modelmaking. Probably the most used by myself is

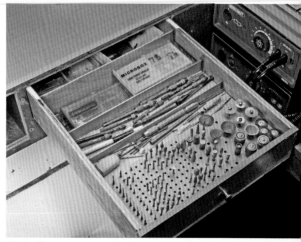

Plate G

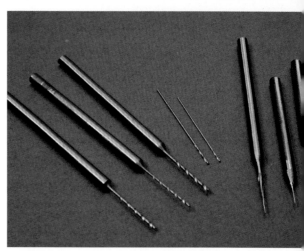

Plate H

Plate I

the rotary handpiece. I would now be lost without one and have for years now made much use of the Minicraft tools depicted in **Plate E**. The smallest in their range is the most useful but the larger one to the back has served me well, fitted with a small grindstone for sharpening home-made drill bits and as a lathe for all those small items not worth setting up the Unimat for, to mention just a couple.

If the Minicraft is a near-essential then the Ram carver shown in **Plate F** is a blatant luxury and while Minicraft are cheap and cheerful, but competent, this handpiece is sheer indulgence. The difference, however, is reflected in the price, and in my opinion it is worth every penny, purely for the pleasure of using it. I doubt you will build better models with it but you will enjoy the process more; definitely a toy for the boys. This is an American tool but I bought mine in the UK and it came with UK voltage. It is very quiet, runs from 0–35,000 revs. is incredibly smooth and totally accurate with its five sealed bearings, reversible and has a quick-release facility for changing burrs. I'm not going to tell you what I paid for it.

Another recent and very useful addition is a second home-made drawer set in the front of my work bench. After several mishaps reaching over a model for the burrs and drills situated at the back of the bench this seemed a sensible option. As can be seen here in **Plate G** my collection of drills, burrs, sanding disks and drums etc. is considerable and I decided they needed better organising – also, it may just save a mast or two in the future.

Plate H shows the various types of drills I use; those on the left have a 2.35mm shank and are suitable for either chuck or collet mounting, and they are readily available in sizes 0.5 to 2.00mm. If you need something finer then twist drills are available down to size 80, they are excellent for most micro drilling requirements, and essential for drilling very fine holes in brass or copper, but on the flip side they break easily and are expensive and I have yet to find a chuck that will grip the finest ones satisfactorily. For general use I find old 2.35mm drill bits that have been sharpened on a grindstone very satisfactory for many tasks. These have the advantage of being easy to reshape and sharpen for different requirements. These are formed as shown in **Plate I**. The old drill bit is mounted in the handpiece and offered up to a small grind wheel as shown, with both in motion. When the desired length and diameter of the tip is

Plate J

Plate K

Plate L

achieved the handpiece is stopped and the tip lightly touched to the wheel, at an angle, on three sides to provide a sharp three-sided cutting tip.

One of the other tools, shown here in **Plate J**, that I would nowadays class as an esential is the Preac saw. It is a beautifully-machined precision tool though it may be of limited use to the warship modeller particularly if a lot of the work is in plastic. Being of American origin it does require a transformer to run it.

From the same stable comes the thickness sander/planer. I run both of them off the same transformer. Here in **Plate K** it can be seen connected to my rather Heath-Robinson dust extractor.

Plate L shows part of the bench in my 'Machine Shop' with the disk sander, a very useful tool for the warship modeller, invaluable for finishing the sides of hulls and superstructures, amongst other tasks.

Also to be seen is part of the dust-extraction system in this room. A vacuum nozzle is 'plugged' into either the flexible hose or the rigid pipe mounted on the timber upright in order to service a variety of machines.

As with many other pieces of equipment, minor or even major adaptations sometimes need to be made to get the best out of them. On this sander I ground away the front edge of the shield curving over the top of the disk until it was set back slightly from the front. Had it been allowed to remain in its original state it would be impossible to sand a straight edge longer than a few inches; a case of good on safety but useless for purpose. Also these machines come with quite a gap between table and disk to allow for tilting, hopeless when working with small items, but nothing a piece of ply and some double-sided tape won't solve.

I bought the scroll saw in **Plate M** fairly recently for a Navy Board model I was working on, and have since found it very useful for a variety of tasks. The blades available mean that it will cope with anything from wood and plastic to metal; it has virtually made redundant the band saw now situated out in the shed.

Plate N. When I first started modelmaking I sharpened tools laboriously with several grades of oilstones, and always hated the things. They are efficient of course but tools and hands get oily, not ideal when working with delicate items made from wood and paper that will at some point need painting with acrylic or enamel paint. So when the diamond wet stones first appeared I was only too pleased to make the change. They work well; but not, it must be

Plate M

Plate N

Plate O

admitted, as well as this machine, I have had it for several years now and it's brilliant. It is a TOMEK SuperGrind, a Swedish machine. It comprises a slow revolving sharpening stone that runs in a trough of water and a leather polishing wheel. There are a selection of jigs available for a variety of tools and blades. It brings my chisels, knives and scalpel blades to a razor-sharp polished finish, making a pleasure out of a chore.

Plate O. Last but not least there is that standby of the modelmaker for many decades now, the Unimat lathe. I have mine rigged here with a separate motor

powering the drill press. It has seen a lot of service over many years.

I have of course many other tools filling boxes and drawers around the place, a lifetime's accumulation. However, most are seldom if ever used and the majority of those shown here could be easily dispensed with. Certainly, for modern warships rather than timber-built sailing vessels the requirements lessen considerably, but I do get pleasure and satisfaction from tools that do the job well and add to the pleasure of the work.

▪ Paints ▪

White Ensign Models (www.whiteensignmodels.com) can provide a complete range of excellent enamel naval colours for the modelmaker. I bought a tin each of their G20 Medium Grey-Green, G45 Pale Grey-Green, B30 Mid Blue-Grey and RN White. I started work on the paintwork using these, but I have for many years now been working with acrylic paints, originally using Humbrol but I have now switched to those marketed by Games Workshop for painting fantasy figures. They are

excellent paints but if you choose to use them it does mean mixing your own colours, quite a time-consuming process. When I had matched mine to the White Ensign ones I took them all down a shade, and even so felt them to be rather too brash when applied to the model, so numerous very thin washes were added to the paintwork as I proceeded. *Caesar* is shown here on completion in October 1944, wearing the Special Home Fleet Destroyer Scheme.

Building
HMS *Caesar*
1944

Those who have seen any of my other books, which take the reader step-by-step through the building of a model, will find that this sequence is not strictly followed in this volume since there are so many different fittings to work on that I or any other modelmaker will frequently switch between one and another as whim or convenience dictate until the time comes for the final assembly, so I have largely divided the text into chapters dealing with each of the major areas or fittings of the ship.

• Hull and Decks •

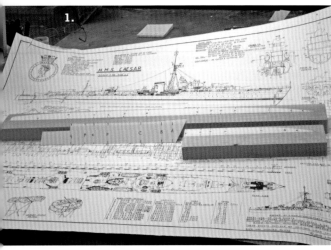

1.

The hull was formed from two blocks of jelutong, one for the full length of hull below the level of the main deck and the other for the forecastle. These can be seen here along with templates that were traced from the plans and cut from 10 thou plastic card. These were then marked with the relevant station lines.

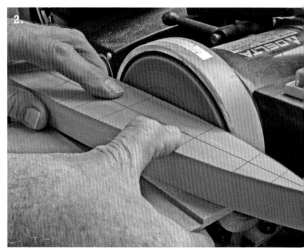

2.

A centreline and the station lines have been drawn on both pieces of timber, then using the templates the plan of the ship was also marked on them before trimming roughly to shape on the band saw. Finishing the job is done on the disk sander.

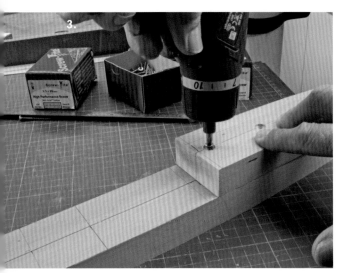

3.

Next the two sections were temporarily screwed together. The holes were pre-drilled and well countersunk.

4.

The profile template was next employed to mark in the stem and the 'centreline' height of the forecastle and main decks. The stem and the forecastle were then trimmed roughly to size on the band saw and the two blocks separated.

5.

Using a small bull-nosed plane, the forecastle was tidied up and levelled down to the line marked in the previous photograph.

6.

If you possess a Unimat lathe or similar, or a drill press, you may find one of these large carbide rotary cutters useful when thicknessing. I have set it in the chuck above the saw table of my Unimat and used the drill lever to lower it to the required height. Now the timber to be thicknessed or levelled can be passed backwards and forwards beneath it for a fast and accurate finish. It is being used here to level the aft section of the forecastle. With this job completed the two sections of the hull are glued and screwed together.

7.

With the top surfaces levelled to the centerline of the decks, the deck edges were marked, as can be seen here, before introducing the camber. Most of this work can be done with the small plane but the area close to the break of the forecastle is best tackled with a chisel.

8.
Finishing off with a sanding board.

9.
Now the sides of the hull are shaped using a violin-maker's plane for the concave surfaces beneath the knuckle . . .

10.
. . . and the bull-nose plane elsewhere.

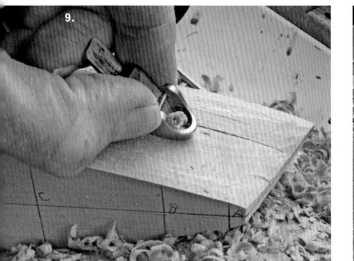

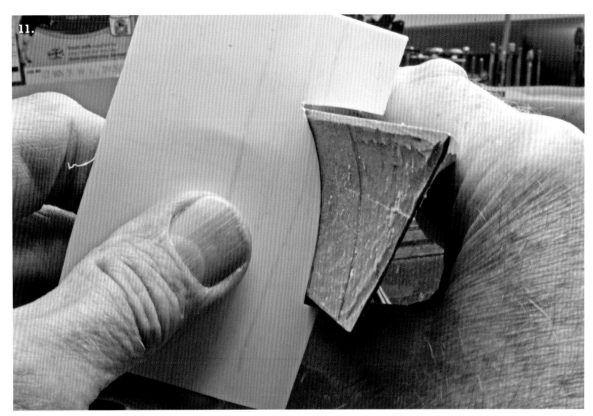

11.

11.
While doing this work it needs to be checked regularly with templates traced from the plans. I cut mine from plastic card, but any fairly rigid and easily-cut material would do.

12.
Once again the final finish was given with a variety of sanding boards, and for the more awkward curves, sandpaper, wrapped around various cylindrical objects. I am using one cut from an old silicone tube and in the background can be seen a pen and a film canister, both of which also make useful formers. When satisfied with the shape and finish of the hull it can be put on one side for a while.

12.

13.

13.
The wood used for the superstructure was also jelutong; cut roughly to size on the table saw out in the shed, then reduced to exactly the right thickness, once again using the method shown in photograph 6. A centreline was then marked in and the plan of the deckhouses established by drawing around a half-breadth template, aligned with the centerline, before turning it over to mark the other side. The final trimming to size is being done on the disk sander.

14.
Once the various superstructure units have been cut to size they are positioned on the hull and held firmly in place while a couple of holes are drilled through them and then on down into the hull a short distance. The drill size needs to be the same as some commercially available, or home-made, dowel rod, the former being easily obtainable from hardware stores; the actual diameter is relatively unimportant.

14.

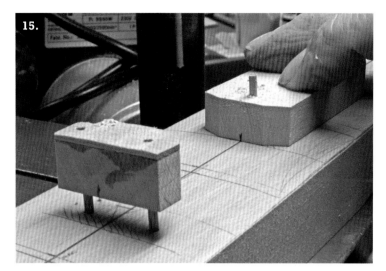

15.
Short lengths of the dowel are cut and inserted through the superstructure and down into the hull, then a little Superglue is run around the top of the dowel before trimming it off flush. This provides easily removable and replaceable superstructures that will always remain accurately aligned and provide a secure fixing when they are finally glued in place on the hull.

16.
At the break of the forecastle a recess has been cut to accept the overlapping section of deck.

17.
Here it can be seen temporarily in place with the superstructure fitted above it. Note the poor join beneath the side of the superstructure. This is due to the camber of the deck and is unimportant as it will eventually be covered with a paper facing.

18.

Now to move on to the decks. I decided early on with this project that I didn't want the smooth and rather bland finish so often given to steel decks. If you go aboard *Cavalier* or *Belfast*, or any warship of this vintage, you are immediately aware of the metal plating with all its overlaps and imperfections, giving a very different feel and texture from one depicted by a smooth sheet of Bristol board or similar. This photograph taken on board *Cavalier* gives a clear idea of the prominence of this feature.

19.

Armed with a selection of on-board photographs and Norman Ough's drawing for a destroyer's deck plating, I marked in the layout on the areas of steel deck; they were then given a couple of coats of Seccotine before starting to lay the plates. This was done working from aft using architects' detail paper. The strip held between my fingers was glued down and then trimmed off where the plate ended; the next was laid slightly overlapping it and so on to the end of the deck. No attempt was made to simulate the overlap between strakes at this stage; they were laid side by side.

20.

The next task was the fitting of the 'Semtex' coating to those areas so treated. I used cartridge paper for this but gave it a couple of coats of paint as a primer before laying it.

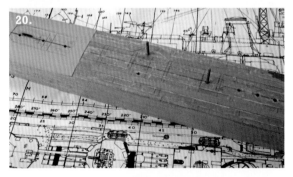

21.

This little tool made from a few scraps of wood provides an ideal way of trimming the 'Semtex' a uniform distance from the side of the ship. The scalpel blade projects just far enough to cut through the cartridge paper.

22.
The trimmer in use.

23.
The next job is laying narrow strips of detail paper over all the longitudinal joins in the plating to simulate the overlaps, and then finally fitting the footstrips fitted to the deck to improve footing on a wet deck. They are fitted in a fore and aft direction in the waist of the ship and port to starboard across the forecastle. Some of those fitted to the waist can be seen quite clearly in the previous photograph.

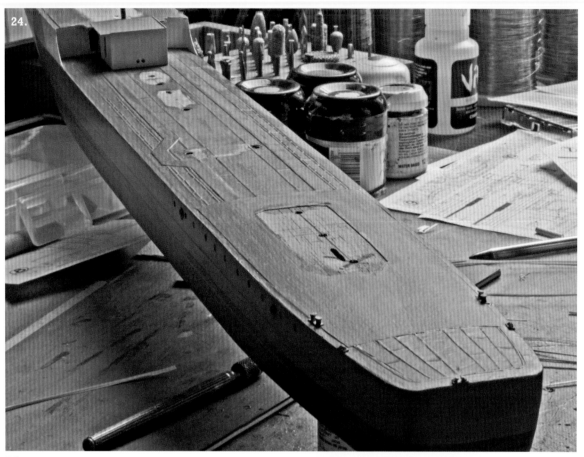

24.
The completed deck after painting. The side
lighting shows the degree of texture that can be
achieved, very different from the bland and
perfectly smooth decks one so often sees even on
quite large-scale models.

25.
Now to move on to the ship's sides; the strakes are
marked in with pencil and then the 'in' strakes
were given several coats of sanding sealer,
rubbing down well between coats. These will need
a grain-free finish as they will not be plated over.

26.

Before proceeding with the plating there was one more detail to be fitted, the curved side plates at the break of the forecastle. This was cut from 1/64in ply and rebated into the hull as shown.

27.

It was finished off with a diamond burr, the join made good with Superglue and then given several coats of the sanding sealer.

28.

Not having tried showing the individual plates at this scale before I was determined to try and do so with *Caesar*. First of all the individual plates of the 'in' strakes were marked and then lightly scored using a steel rule and scalpel. Then using a sharp chisel as shown here the aft side of the score was depressed a fraction to give the impression of an overlapping plate.

29.

Now the 'out' strakes are added using a fairly thin paper and white woodworking glue. When dry they were also given a coat of sanding sealer and the individual plates marked on them. They were then given the same treatment as shown in the previous photograph for the 'in' strakes.

30.

The ship's side on the finished model. I think the realism created by correctly plating the hull far outweighs the extra time spent on the work.

31.

All the superstructure and bridge decks were cut from 1/64in ply; they were glued to their superstructures only after these had been given the required camber. In the photograph are templates for the bridge deck and superstructure deck. The latter is also in the process of being cut out from the ply. As can be seen I am including the forward blast screen with this deck, all the fold lines having been scored from below.

32.

The blast screen roughly cut to shape and being held in place with strips of masking tape while checking the angles with this ply jig.

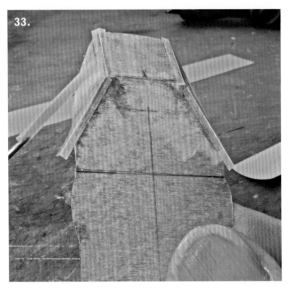

33.
When satisfied that the angles are all correct the
rather fragile folds were flooded with Superglue
and reinforced with strips of detail paper. When
dry these were sanded down to blend with the
underside of the shield.

34.
The reinforcing baffles being fitted. I must have
spent many hours researching the exact shape and
layout of these. Exact details being unavailable, I
relied heavily on photographic information.

35.

The blast screens nearing completion. They are topped by T bars formed from paper strip.

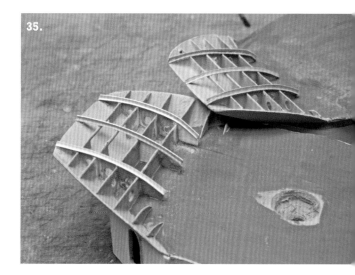

35.

36.

Although a most unlikely scenario in real life I had all the watertight doors open on the model. I feel this helps to develop a 3-D quality, the various doors opening up to the space within. In order to create this illusion the superstructures had to be opened up from below, a much easier proposition then building a hollow structure, particularly when using the easily-worked jelutong. The first step is to drill a series of holes over the area to be removed.

36.

37.

Now, using first of all a carbide cutter and then a diamond burr, the inner area is brought to a fine finish and the door opening made slightly larger all round than the finished doorway; when finished the inside can be painted a dark grey.

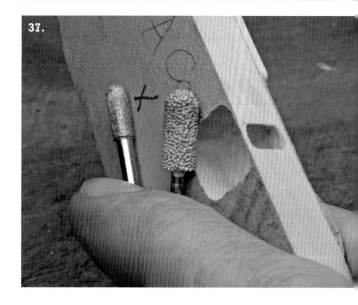

37.

38.
Next the facings for the various deck houses are cut to size and the watertight doors marked on them, making sure that they exactly correspond to those already cut in the superstructures. They are then cut out; I find it helpful to use a small punch for the corners as shown here before removing the remainder with a scalpel.

39.
After the facings have been glued to the super-structures a paper rim is fitted to the openings.

40.
The watertight doors being cut from thin Bristol board. Two rectangles will be needed for each, one slightly smaller than the other.

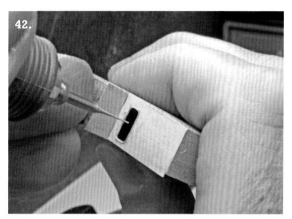

41.
The two rectangles glued together and the reinforcing bars being fitted.

42.
Using one of the fine home-made drill bits, holes are drilled for the door clips.

43.
The clips were simply made from right-angles of copper wire glued in place with a spot of Superglue. This photograph shows one of the first watertight doors to be fitted at the break of the forecastle. Alongside it is one of the openings in the superstructure; noticeably larger than the door opening that will cover it.

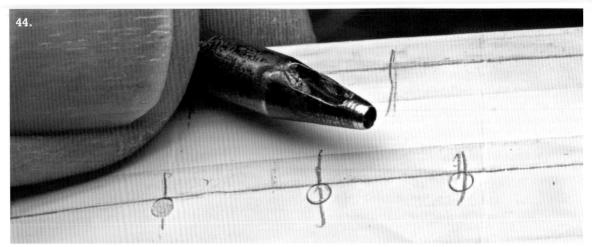

44.

44.

There are a fair number of scuttles to be fitted to *Caesar*. This is my preferred method of making them. A line has been drawn where the top of a row of scuttles are to be located and marks made along that line where the individual ones will be fitted. Then using a punch of the required size they are lightly punched using only hand pressure.

I have quite a collection of punches now. Many of them, including this one, are home-made on my Unimat lathe. If you have access to a lathe they are easily turned from silver steel and hardened by heating to a cherry red and plunging in oil, though I have several that have done me good service over the years turned from 4in and 6in nails, remaining untempered. I also possess a number of commercially-made ones. They are available if you hunt around, but I find they usually need sharpening for the fine work I require of them.

45.

Now take a drill shank and clean up the end on a stone, mount it in some form of handle or a pin vice and firmly depress the punched circles as shown.

I prepare disks for the glass by giving a sheet of paper several coats of very dark grey gloss paint, gently rubbing down between coats until a high gloss finish is achieved; then as many disks as will be required are punched from it using the same punch. These are then glued in place with a little white glue, but only of course at a later stage when the final painting of the model has been completed.

45.

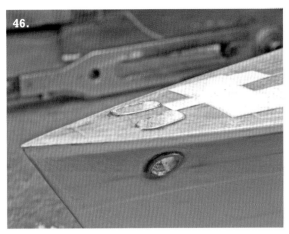

46.
Before starting to detail the decks the hawsehole needs to be fashioned. This is a fairly straightforward job that involves making and fitting the brass or copper rings and gluing them in place on the hull and deck, and then with increasingly larger drills and burs opening it up. There is usually some unwanted damage done to the inside of the opening but this is easily remedied with filler smoothed on with the shank of a drill bit.

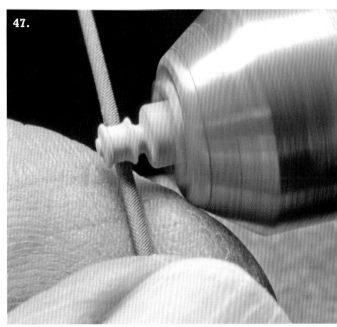

47.
The capstans were turned in the Minicraft drill from boxwood; a short spigot should be left underneath for fitting.

48.
The remainder of the capstan gear has been made from boxwood and paper. Paper has also been used to fit the rather unusual curved breakwater; it took a fair bit of trial and error to get this fitting cut to shape in one piece. Some of the foot strips mentioned earlier are in the process of being fitted.

49.
The forward end of the ship at about this stage, looking decidedly empty and bleak. It is just possible to make out the wire rim that has now been fitted to the top edge of the breakwater.

▪ The Bridge ▪

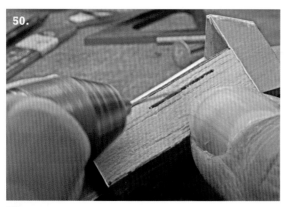

50.

The bridge superstructure was formed from a block of jelutong with a second wedge-shaped section added above it to form the front of the bridge. The deck (incorporating the bridge wings and the extension to the rear) was cut from 1/32in ply and glued in place before covering the sides with very thin card. Before gluing the sides in place a groove was cut, or rather drilled, as seen here for the searchlight platforms, the drilling being done from various directions until the slot was opened up.

51.

The side plating being checked for fit beneath the bridge wings and over the slot for the searchlight platforms.

52.

The bridge seen from aft during construction. All the side plating has been fitted and along most of its top the wind deflectors have been added, all the component parts being cut from paper, glued in place with diluted white glue before finally reinforcing with thin Superglue. Just forward of the director control tower (DCT) can be seen the canopy over the hatch to the deck below; before fitting the deck this hatch was opened up and the area below it hollowed out and a ladder fitted.

53.
The front of the bridge; the salient feature here not clearly seen in the previous photograph is the screen at the front of the bridge; the front and sides were built from some fairly stiff acetate and the framing for the windows added from pre-painted paper.

53.

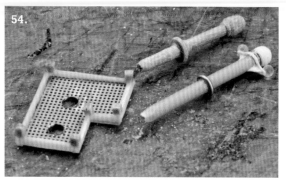

54.

Now to run through some of the bridge fittings. The gyro compass was turned from boxwood and the magnetic compass made from plastic rod; a short section of plastic tube was glued to one end and it was carefully turned to a spherical shape in the Minicraft drill using sandpaper. This has to be done gently or the friction will generate enough heat to melt the plastic. The remainder of the details were made from plastic card, apart from the anti-magnetic spheres which were glass beads. An alternative would be tiny pieces of Milliput rolled into spheres. The base of the compass was formed from a ring of copper wire. On the left can be seen the underside of the etched brass grating these two items were mounted on: the framing and feet were cut from boxwood.

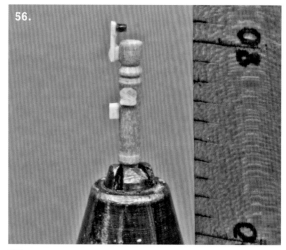

56.

Two sights, to be seen either side of the bridge, were turned from boxwood and detailed with plastic card and rod. The divisions on the rule to the right are in 16ths of an inch.

55.

A number of sights of various types are required: there are two of this type for the rear of the bridge plus one either side on the searchlight platforms. Their construction is quite straightforward using wire, plastic rod and plastic card.

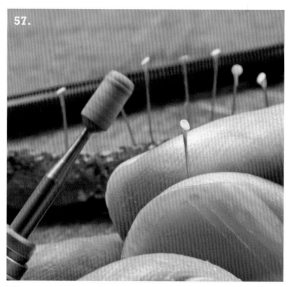

57.

There are a seemingly endless number of voice pipes required for the bridge and emergency control position. I find this method of making them is as good as any. Little circles of paper or card have been punched out and have been Superglued to short lengths of wire at an angle. They are then built up beneath the disks with several more applications of glue before being finally cleaned up and reduced to an oval shape with a small stone.

58.

The DCT was a fairly straightforward structure to build. It is basically formed from a block of boxwood mounted on a turned boxwood cylinder. The detailing is added using paper and plastic card as shown. There are a couple of features warranting further description: firstly there is the very top of the control tower. This was made from Perspex with the sides highly polished with metal polish. The second, and these are details that will be found throughout the ship, are the ladders. For most of my earlier models these were formed on a wooden jig as will be explained later in the book, but I now use some of my own etched brass ladders. On their own they appear very flat and lacking in three dimensions, but with the addition of a length of copper wire glued over the uprights they give a very passable imitation of a properly-built ladder at this scale.

59.

Slightly further on; now the purpose of the polished sides of the Perspex becomes clear. With the windows and other openings fitted it is possible to glimpse light from the far side, giving the illusion of a hollow tower.

60.

This photograph of the bridge shows many of the fittings described above on the finished model. The Type 285 radar array mounted above the tower consists of paper dishes with wire central poles projecting from them. These are crossed by shorter lengths of thinner wire and once again these were made on a wire jig as described in photograph 178. The remaining wires extending from the dishes almost to the ends of the poles (four to each pole) were very fine and I cannot pretend they were easy to fit. The supporting structure was constructed from a mix of wire and paper. The canopy supports over the bridge were thin card saturated with Superglue fitted to wire supports.

Around the top of the splinter plating, where not fitted with wind deflectors, a thin wire rim has been glued on the outside of the top edge. This feature will be in evidence in all the final photographs on all superstructure decks: it is one of those little details that really make a difference to the authentic appearance of a finished model.

▪ The Funnel ▪

61.

There are many ways of making warship funnels, for instance carving from solid before hollowing out from above to casting the two sides from ABS or Plasticard. The latter method I have used in the past very successfully, however with this model I determined to try something slightly different and use paper instead. As can be seen here the first task is to make a former to the inside dimensions of the funnel, checking carefully along its length with a template.

62.

The former is then given several coats of candle wax, with a light application of heat from a naked flame to melt the wax between coats, thus ensuring a good smooth non-stick surface. Now two layers of good-quality paper are held around the former as seen here and then given a good coating of very thin Superglue, which will soak through the layers of paper. When dry and removed from the former the two sides will be found to be quite strong and resilient.

63.

Using a sharp blade the surplus can now be carefully trimmed away.

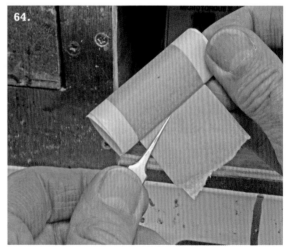

64.

I next glued the two halves together and added another layer, this time using some Gumstrip sealing tape.

65.

Just to ensure maximum strength I have glued some thin paper strips along the joins both inside and out. The outside ones have been sanded to blend in with the Gumstrip.

The lower casing for the funnel has a pronounced flare to it so it will be incorporated in the plug forming the base of the funnel. The profile for this was transferred from the plans and shaped as shown here.

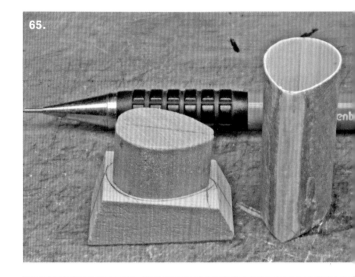

66.

The funnel casing was then held firmly in place on the plug and the lower casing roughed out with a sanding disk . . .

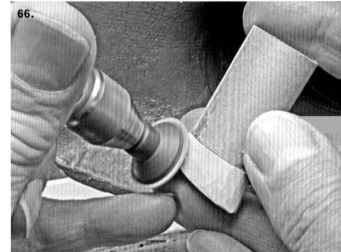

67.

. . . before being cleaned up with sanding boards.

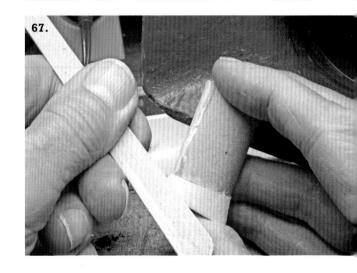

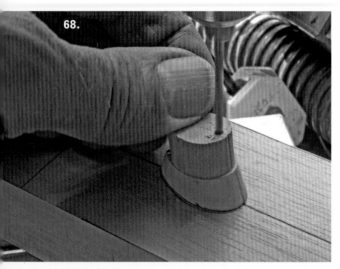

68.
When the finish was satisfactory it was positioned on the hull and two holes drilled through the plug and down into the deck.

69.
Dowels have now been fitted and the funnel can now be fitted and removed at will until final assembly.

70.
With the upper and lower sections of the funnel permanently joined it was plated with strips of Gumstrip to represent the individual metal plates. What is not apparent is that when finished most of the joins were all but invisible so they were emphasised by scoring with a knife.

71.
The plated funnel. It now has an inner casing of paper glued inside the top and in the foreground is the hood; this was cut from Plasticard and it is a tight fit over the inner casing. The flange, already fitted to the base of the funnel, was fashioned in the same way as the hood. To the right of the picture is a former for the cage. A length of wire that will form the rim of the cage has been shaped around the punch that can be seen in the background and is lying loosely in place on the former.

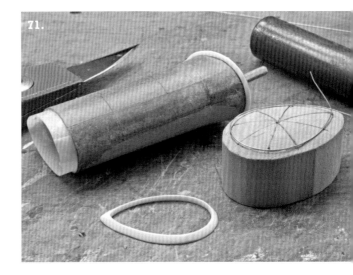

72.
The rim has now been taped in place with some narrow strips of Sellotape and the remainder of the cage has been formed by winding the wire tightly around the former; then, while being held firmly in the vise, the joins were soldered.

73.
The siren platform was supported by these five wires inserted in holes drilled in the casing. These are left over-length as they will later be bent upwards to form the rail stanchions, the two wires forming the sides of the platform having been glued to them.

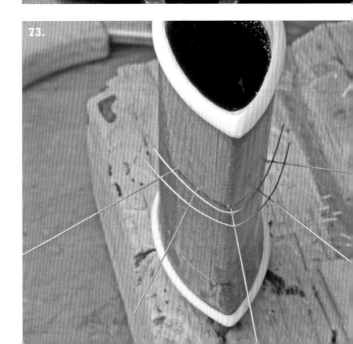

74.

Individual strips of wire have been cut and glued across them to form the platform grating and a narrow strip of paper glued to the outside edge.

There are three uptakes fitted to the outside of the funnel, two at the front, just visible at the base and the one seen clearly here behind the platform; it was quite a game fitting it at this stage. It should have been done before starting work on the platform, but these things happen – a lot.

75.

With the funnel finished and the sirens fitted it just remains to fit the cage, a process only half completed in this picture. I find the best way to go about this rather delicate task is as follows. Firstly the cage must be cut away from the former, leaving long-enough ends to be fitted to the funnel as shown here. Now these ends should be bent sharply underneath the cage so that it will rest on top of the hood in its correct and final position. Holding the cage firmly in the tweezers and resting their very point on the hood for stability, another pair of tweezers are used to bend the ends down inside the funnel, which are then glued to the inside of the hood with Superglue, applied with a wire as demonstrated.

▪ The Mast ▪

76.

I had been looking forward to building this complex but visually fascinating structure, though not, I must admit, without a considerable degree of trepidation. I had originally intended to make a fine wire skeleton and build on to this with paper strips and angles, relying on Superglue to stiffen and strengthen things up a bit. I was, however, rather worried about the fragility and vulnerability of a mast made in this fashion, particularly during the final assembly and rigging, so sought an alternative. I eventually came across some brass angle and strip of just the right dimensions. Problem solved, but I still expected the job to be one of the trickier ones on the model. Conversely, as often happens, it proved to be one of the most straightforward, comparatively problem-free and enjoyable.

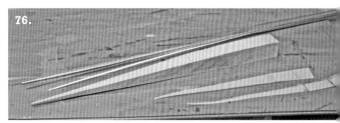

76.

A hardwood former was made to the inside dimensions of the mast and then all the horizontal straps cut and fitted to it with narrow strips of Sellotape, keeping this well clear of the corners. Now the four angle sections for the uprights were bound in place with wire and the joints soldered, whereupon the jig, having fulfilled its purpose, can be withdrawn. Needless to say all the areas to be soldered had been cleaned up and a little flux applied during the assembly.

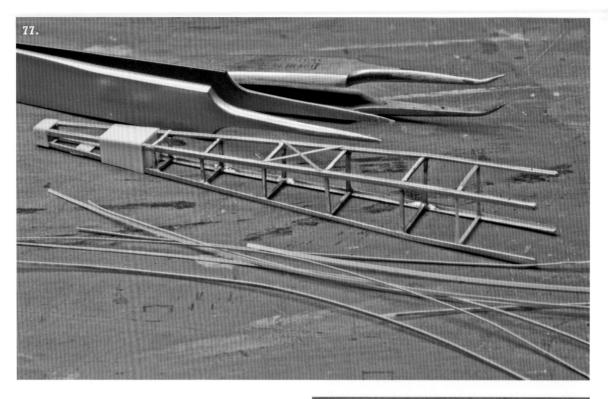

77.

77.
The now quite-rigid structure can be added to and build up with a variety of media. Paper strips are here being fitted to form some of the diagonals.

78.

78.
The remainder of the work is fairly straightforward model construction. The pole mast and spar were made from brass rod and the ladders are brass etchings, the majority of the other details are fabricated from wire and paper. The one real brain-teaser is the HF/DF aerial at the mast head, and this certainly does warrant further description.

79.

Before taking on this project I had never before built or taken any real note of one of these aerials so when first examining plans and photographs of these ships was somewhat confused by what I was seeing. The plans and some of the ships' photographs showed an aerial like the one on the right, other photographs one as shown on the left. I am sure anyone in the know will think me incredibly uninformed and naïve, and I wouldn't blame them. They are of course the very same aerial but seen from different directions. Obvious when the penny drops.

79a.

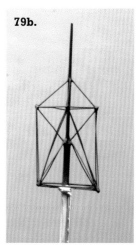

79b.

80.

This photograph of the HF/DF aerial taken during construction shows clearly how the illusion occurs. The aerial is built around two squares of wire, the upper one measuring from corner to corner the same as the lower one from side to side and they are set at 45 degrees to one another: once this is realised all becomes clear. It looks quite a fearsome structure to assemble in miniature but in practice was fairly simple. The first wires to be fitted were the four radiating outwards from the base, then the lower square was made up from one length of wire and laid on top of them, glued, and the ends trimmed off with the scissors. Next the four wires from the corners of the lower square to the centre of the aerial were carefully cut to size and fitted, forming in effect a pyramid. Now, four wires, counterparts to the ones just fitted, are cut over-long and glued to the centre radiating upwards to form the corners of an inverted pyramid sitting tip to tip above the first. The second square can now be made and fitted after adjusting the four wires to ensure the square sits at the correct height and centrally over the mast so forming the base of the inverted pyramid. With this solid structure in place the remainder of the work is comparatively easy and should be clear from the photographs.

80.

▪ The Armament ▪

The armament for *Caesar* proved to be a lengthy project in its own right, not only for the actual time spent constructing of the various mountings – in fact this proved to be relatively straightforward – but because of the time spent accumulating, assimilating and analysing the information required to build them. It is one thing to have a set of plans and a few photographs of a mounting and quite another to construct a reasonably accurate miniature representation of it, particularly when the mountings are as complex as the 4.5in guns, or even more so with the Hazemeyer Bofors. The Lambert drawings are brilliant and will give masses of information. But they are drawn to an extremely large scale and they are of the gun mountings themselves and not angled towards the modelmaker, so additional information in the form of photographs was needed. I made a first ever visit to the Explosion! Museum of naval ordnance at Gosport where I took a great many photographs that proved invaluable while working on the model, and at the same time took in the Submarine Museum a short distance away. I also had some photographs taken a year previously on board HMS *Cavalier* at Chatham: despite the changes and refits there was still much of interest and use. Should you be contemplating a model warship of the Second World War and have not already done so, visit these museums, if for no other reason than to 'set the scene' and get a feeling for these ships and the weapons that armed them.

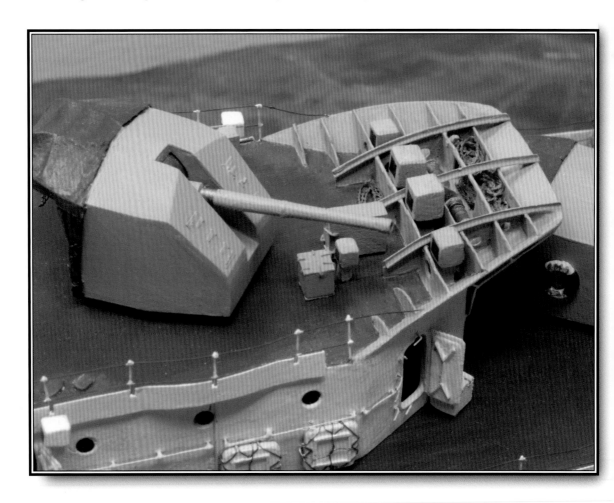

▪ The 4.5in Guns ▪

Here is a quartet of photographs of gun mountings, the top two are of *Cavalier*'s 4.5in, and the lower two are similar mountings at the Explosion Museum. These and the many others I took, along with the Lambert drawings, provided all the information I needed for *Caesar*'s main armament. As can be seen only one of them now retains the canvas hood and curtains that *Caesar* will be fitted with. Before starting work time has to be spent trying to understand the essential components of the mounting in order to decide which to include and which to leave out. When reducing a 9ft-high

gun mounting to little more than half-an-inch high compromises have to be made, obviously. The question is which ones and how? I wish I had a black and white answer to this. I tried reducing the Lambert drawings to 16ft to 1in on the computer and printing the result; this was of limited assistance as all the fine detail disappeared into a blur. I tend to tackle items like this from the centre out, starting with the barrel, breech block and mounting, then work my way outwards from the centre adding increasingly fine detail until ability or common sense tell me to stop.

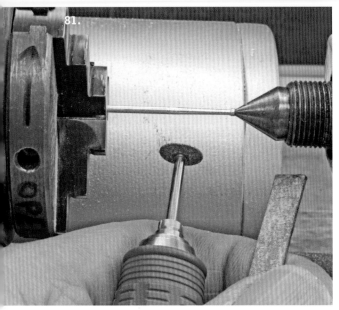

81.
The first task to tackle was the barrels. These were turned from fine aluminium tubing I had, fortunately of just the right diameter. However, it was too delicate to turn in the traditional way and the initial shaping was done with a disk-shaped diamond burr, finishing off with a fine file.

82.
Square blocks were next made from plastic card and drilled to accept the barrels. These will form the square section between the barrel and breech blocks.

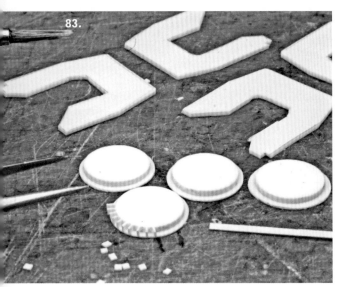

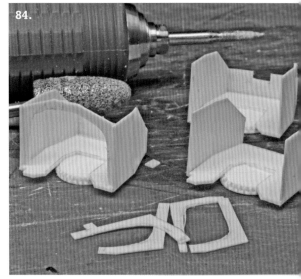

83.
The base rings were cut from plastic card as were the individual lugs. All were assembled with liquid cement. The platforms for the gun shields have also been cut from plastic card.

84.
The sides of the shield being assembled. I am using th burrs to further define the curved openings in the bac the shield.

85.

Taking shape. Building up the framework in this way brings the model closer to its prototype but the main reason for doing so is to strengthen the whole structure and make the fitting of the final plates easier and more accurate.

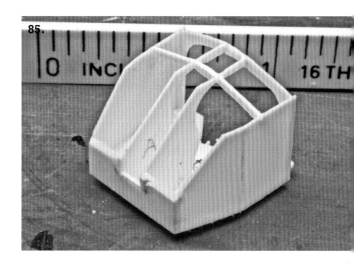

86.

The final sections of the plating are being added to the shields and a basic structure for the mounting has been made. The barrels have been glued in place, breech blocks made and fitted and the trunnion ends added. It is important at this stage to ensure that the guns are an accurate fit inside the shields. If there are any problems they are best resolved before detailing the mounting further.

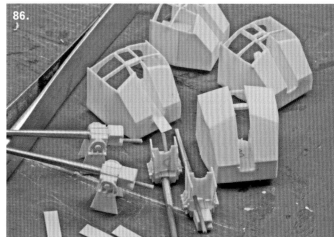

87.

The mantlet plates were formed by drawing strips of plastic card firmly over the edge of a steel rule. They were then drilled to accept the barrel and each gun fitted temporarily to its shield. When the plates lined up perfectly inside the front of the shield, and the gun mountings sat exactly in position on the bases, a drop of Superglue was applied to the barrel to fix the mantlet plate permanently in place. The mountings can then be removed from the shields for final detailing. However, at this point I marked each shield and mounting to ensure that on final assembly the original pairing remained the same. Note a few extra details have been added including the counterbalance weight and its supporting arm.

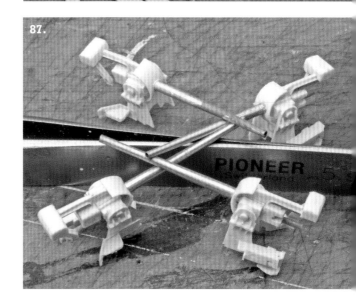

88.
Further details being added including the fuse-setting gear, loading tray and seats for the gun crews.

89.
The 'collar' around the barrels abutting the mantle plates was formed from plastic card. A strip was held as shown around a section of the aluminium tubing used for the barrels; it was then gently heated by passing it through a lighter flame, allowed to cool, and then cut into sections.

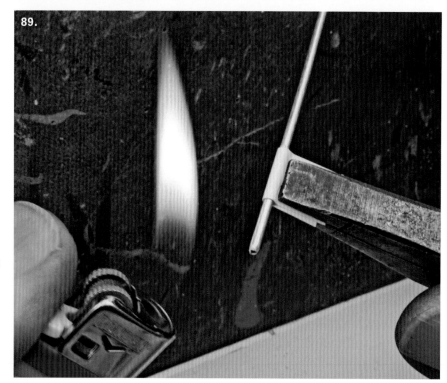

90.

90.
The 'collars' fitted along with the sealing ring halfway along the barrels and the thickening at the muzzle, these latter two being cut from thin paper. The remaining detail has been added to both guns and mountings; each of these would be impossible to name and demonstrate being fitted, but I have endeavoured to show the guns from a variety of angles to give a clear picture of the process.

91.
I decided to make the canvas canopies from tissue-paper, and rather than build wire frames and attempt to cover them I took the reverse approach, forming the covers first and then fitting the main struts of the framework after the canopies were fitted to the shields.

A mould was carved from a scrap of wood and the wire framework glued to it with Superglue. This was then liberally coated with candle wax, melting it on with a few passes of the lighter flame.

91.

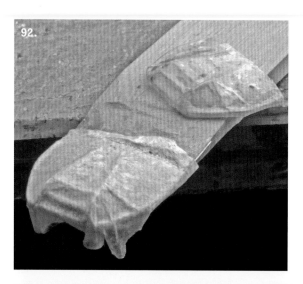

92.

The canopies were formed from two layers of tissue-paper. The first one was draped over the mould while wet, dried off with a hair dryer, liberally coated with glue and the second one bedded down on top. When dry it was removed from the mould and trimmed to size. I tried several different glues, but although most of them worked fine, I found Seccotine the best, but gave the finished canopies a coat of thin Superglue for good measure.

93.

The completed gun shields and canopies. I used an airbrush to apply the paint but a brush would have done the job just as well. It would just have taken a lot longer.

94.

One of the guns fitted to its shield.

95.

95.
The canopies being fitted to the shields. Before painting the shields I had fitted a narrow strip of masking tape along the top of the shields. These are now removed to provide a clean surface for gluing the canopies to. Before the canopies are fitted the side curtains need to be made and fixed in place. These were made from pre-painted tissue-paper.

96.

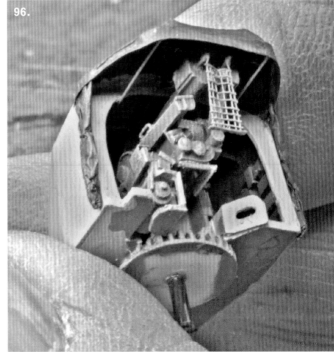

96.
A completed mounting with the canopy.

▪ The Hazemayer Bofors ▪

I was initially looking forward to building this complex mounting. I didn't expect it to be a simple undertaking but I felt the complexity would add to the interesting nature of the work as well as the appearance of the completed model. I had copies of John Lambert's plans for the mounting, but as I mentioned above these were very large scale and extremely detailed; I also had a good selection of, unfortunately, rather poor quality photographs of

Hazemeyers, most of which were of little use as they showed little or no detail suitable for use as reliable reference, being taken from ships' portraits and blown up on the computer screen. There are also seemingly many variations and marks which further complicates things. There is a very good close up of *Caesar's* Hazemeyer platform in *Profile 32* on the 'Ca' class and photographs and drawings in *Destroyer Weapons* and *Scale Model Warships*.

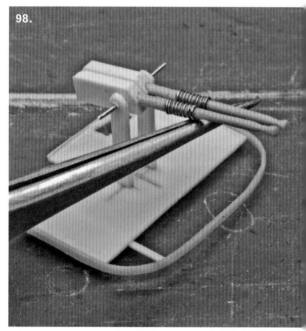

97.
The base plate for the mounting incorporates a free-standing curved rail; I made this from a strip of thin card. A scrap of wood was shaped to the inside dimensions of the base and a strip of double sided tape applied to its edge. The card was then held in place as shown and liberally flooded with thin Superglue. This was allowed to soak into the card after which any surplus is quickly wiped away. When dry it will be quite rigid and maintain its shape.

98.
Barrels have been turned from boxwood and the breech blocks cut from plastic card. I could not ascertain the correct shape or structure of the uprights supporting the barrels as both in the plans and photographs they are obscured by the surrounding detail, so I contented myself with getting the height above the base of the mounting right. This proved not to be a problem, however, since, as in the plans and photographs, this feature was eventually lost amidst a sea of detail. Until nearing completion I left the barrels to freely elevate on their wire trunnions. This gave the opportunity of viewing the mounting on the completed model before deciding finally how I wished it to appear.

99.
The various raised platforms and the cross-level unit to the front of the mount have been added along with other features that I had managed to visually identify. Most of the mounting will be made from plastic card though small amounts of paper, card and wire are used where appropriate.

100.
Some copper wire has been filed down to a D section and has been used to simulate the spent cartridge chutes. They have not yet been trimmed to size. The range unit has been fitted to the left of the platform and elevating gear either side of the trunnions.

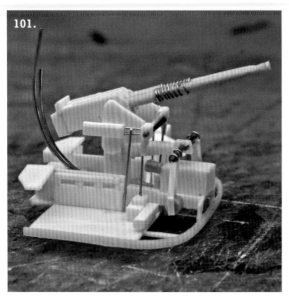

101.

Here and in the previous photograph can be seen – to the front of the mounting – the rather complex counterbalance mechanism with the attendant weights.

102.

More details being added including the seats for the various gun trainers and operators. The framework for the radar is also in the process of being erected.

103.

On the nearside of the mounting can be seen the remote training tube unit and just to the right and slightly to the front of it the cooling water tank. Just to the side of the trunnion can be seen the training sight and in the same position on the far side of the barrels the layer's sight.

104.

Nearing completion. In the foreground are the various components for the radar aerial which like the barrels have to be made so that they can be elevated or depressed as they will obviously need to be set at the same angle as the barrels.

105.

105.
The aerials in place and the whole mounting ready for the airbrush. This is one fitting that I would not relish painting by hand.

106.
These three views of the Hazemeyer after airbrushing should give a good impression not only of the complexity of this mounting but also hopefully a sort of visual three-dimensional blueprint for would-be builders of one. Imperfect it may be but the photographs should provide rather more to go on than I was able to unearth; used, of course, as always with the best information <u>you</u> are able to unearth. Beware Chinese whispers.

107.
The front of the mounting giving a clear view of the counterbalance weights and their attendant supports. Just behind the nearside one can be seen the some of the gunlayer's gear, footrests and seat and just above the sight and hand-crank.

108.
A view of the rear with, on the nearside, the barrel water cooling header tank, in the centre the radar switching unit and above, mounted on the rails, the ready-use ammunition lockers.

109.
The completed Hazemeyer mounted on the model. Before final fitting the various platforms and the barrel run-out springs have been give a wash of very dark grey. Also, but not evident in this photograph, the openings in the end of the barrels have been painted black – I shied away from drilling such tiny barrels. Finally I gave the whole mounting, a bit at a time, a wash over with a very dilute and very dark grey, allowing it to flood into any recesses and corners, following up with a little dry brushing with a paler grey. This is not a technique I make general use of so it needs to be done discreetly. It does however help to define the detail work on this very prominent fitting. Surrounding the gun are four ammunition lockers, made from boxwood with thick paper doors and wire clips. On the other side of the platform is the crew's shelter with a tissue-paper curtain; not clearly evident in this picture is the fact that this is blowing in the wind to give just a glimpse of the interior.

▪ The Oerlikons ▪

After the Hazemeyer these little guns were a pleasurable break, being fairly straightforward to construct. As they are so much simpler, not only are the drawings much easier to follow but photographs are easy to interpret, with all the detail, or most of it anyway, being visible. Also a diligent search should turn up a lot more visual reference than I was able to find for the Hazemeyer. *Caesar* will be carrying two single mountings and two doubles.

110.
The barrels for both mountings were basically the same and were turned from brass rod in the large Minicraft drill. This can be started using a sanding disk or diamond burr but needs to be finished with a very fine file.

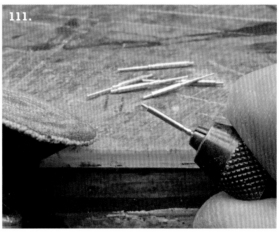

111.
The barrels were then mounted in a pin chuck and the breech end of the gun partially squared off using a sanding disk in a rotary tool.

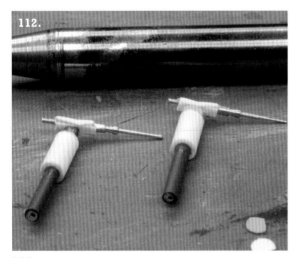

112.
The pedestals for the singles were made from plastic rod and tube and the cradles from plastic card.

113.
The supports for the cradle added.

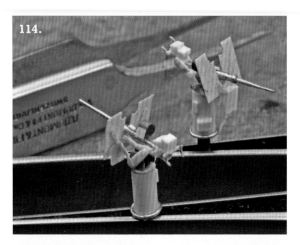

114.
The completed singles; the pedestals have been detailed with plastic card and copper wire hoops, the breech blocks have been fitted and above them the Mk 14 gunsights. The splinter shields with their supports have been cut from thick paper reinforced with thin Superglue; the magazines have been cut from plastic rod and power units fitted to the front of the gunshields

115.
The single mountings in place on the searchlight platform. The raised step around each was fabricated from thin card.

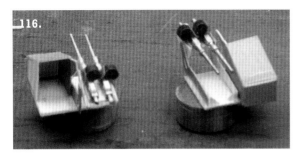

116.
The twin mountings are again fairly basic structures and their fabrication should be quite easy to follow from these photographs. The bases were turned from boxwood and the remainder of the structure in this photograph made from thin card, apart from the magazines which were once more cut from plastic rod.

117.
This photograph should give a good view of the twin mounting on completion, the unpainted state helping to show the different materials used. The inside of the shields have been detailed with plastic card and wire used for the sights, hoops of wire have again been used for the rims at top and bottom of the bases.

118.
One of the completed twins on the starboard bridge wing.

▪ The Torpedo Tubes ▪

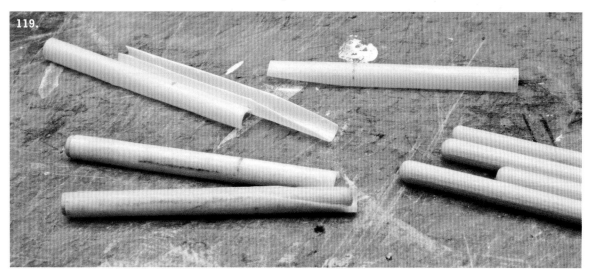

119.

119.
The torpedoes were made from dowel; this was home-produced from a strip of boxwood that was firstly run down on the Preac saw, then the corners planed off by hand and the dowels finished by drawing them through successively smaller holes in a drill gauge. I bought the gauge I use for this purpose nearly forty years ago and have been using it for making dowels of all sizes ever since; it makes a quite acceptable drawplate and if I need anything smaller than a size 60 dowel I use a home-made one made from a piece of tin plate that will take me down to size 80. Making dowels of various sizes is a skill worth mastering whatever sphere of ship modelling you specialise in. So, to get back to the torpedoes, correct lengths were cut from the dowel and were one by one chucked in the large Minicraft drill and the ends rounded off. The tubes were made by taking a strip of the dowel, waxing it liberally with candle wax and then holding two small sheets of paper around it with Superglue between them. When set they will retain their shape and will not stick to the waxed dowel, only your fingers. They can be given a further coat of thin Superglue on both sides before trimming them to shape as seen in this photograph.

120.
The bases for the mountings were cut from boxwood and the reinforcing rings and the flanges joining front and rear sections of the tubes formed by winding some copper wire round a drill shank and cutting off individual hoops. They were then flattened by placing them one at a time on the handle of the square, placing the steel bar on top of it and giving the bar a sharp blow with the hammer; obviously any two fairly heavy and flat objects would do as well. The torpedoes can then be glued inside their tubes and the tubes glued to the bases.

120.

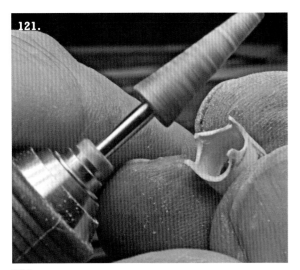

121.
The enclosed blast screen was formed from thin paper wound round a waxed drill shank with just a touch of Superglue applied. After removing it from the drill shank it was flooded with the thin Superglue and, when dry, shaped with this ruby burr to fit over the tubes.

122.
The tubes fitted to the bases: note they are fitted in pairs with a wider gap between the centre two. The blast screen has been temporarily fitted to the tubes to check for fit.

123.
This drill has been sharpened on the TOMEK grinder into a fine chisel point. This and the craft knife were used to remove the sighting windows in the blast shields.

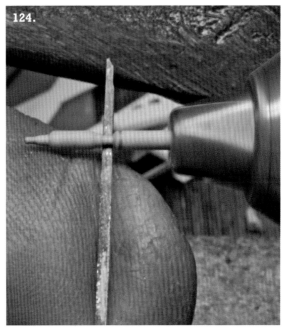

124.
The explosion chambers were turned from boxwood, once again using the fixed Minicraft drill; they were roughed out with a diamond burr and finished with a fine file.

125.
Fitting the explosion chambers; holes have been drilled in them and two short lengths of wire fitted to each. They are being fitted to the pre-drilled holes in the tubes. Small rings of wire are fitted to the rear one, as can be seen here, to form a flange; this will be further built up with white glue to form the inlet to the tube. The rear doors were punched from thin card, burnished on the inside to produce a slightly domed shape and have been fitted with clips, hinges etc. made from wire and paper.

126.
Beginning to take shape; the blast shield is permanently fitted as are the wire flanges. The footplates were cut from thin card and a fine wire rim fitted to all the exposed edges at the front of the mounting.

127.
Nearing completion, the tops of the shields were made by burnishing to produce the domed shape, the hand training platforms and handles have been fitted either side of the mountings and much other fine detail has been added. The detailing to the rear doors is clearly seen in this photograph.

128.
The construction of the torpedo-loading davits should be clear from this photograph. The plinth was turned from a scrap of beech; this was mounted on a paper disk base. The arm of the davit has a card centre faced with paper. All the detail fittings are wire, paper or plastic rod.

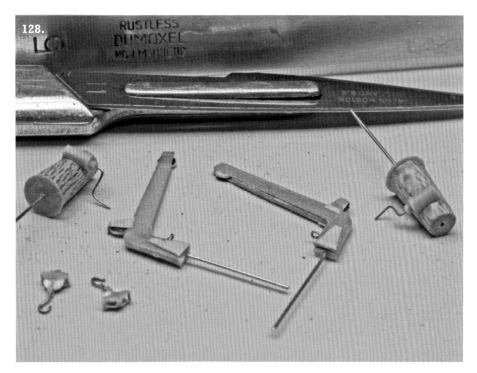

129.
A finished set of torpedo tubes and its davit.

▪ Boats and Rafts ▪

I did not take any photographs of the process of moulding the hulls for the ship's boats but am interpolating a few from a previous work. The only difference is that I was using a grey ABS instead of polystyrene: the process remains identical.

130.

130.
First of all a wooden hull is carved from some fine-grained hardwood, using, as with the ship itself, templates for plan, profile and section. This is carved 'over deep' and with a reasonable wedge of wood left above the sheer line. Screws are then inserted in the top of the hull to form handles.

Next, a cardboard tray is made to contain the filler used for the female mould; the inner drawer from a matchbox is ideal. The wooden male mould is now rubbed over with candle wax, the tray filled with car body filler and the male mould pressed into it until the filler is just above the sheer line. A little gentle pressure should be kept on the tops of the screws until the filler starts to go off to make sure that the wooden hull does not tend to float upwards. When set the hull is worked free from the filler and then sanded down all round so that when replaced in the female mould it leaves a gap of about 10–15 thou. The moulds are then ready for use.

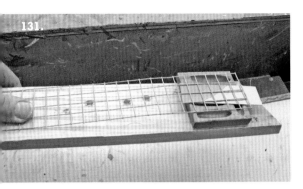

131.

The casting of hulls in either ABS or plastic card is really quite simple, though you may find that some practice is required, and that several castings for each hull are needed before you are satisfied with the result. In practice, a sheet of plastic is placed over the waxed mould and this is held under an electric grill until the plastic softens and sags. Not always as simple as it sounds as the plastic sheet will initially try to roll itself into a cylinder or convolute in some other way, anything other than lie flat the way you want it to, so I have taken to holding it flat with a strip of wire mesh, as shown in this picture, at least in the initial stages of softening.

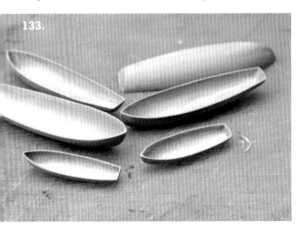

133.

Once the required numbers of castings have been taken they can be trimmed to size and thoroughly cleaned up to remove any traces of wax. I usually use an old stiff-bristled paintbrush, starting out with white spirit and finishing up with hot water and detergent.

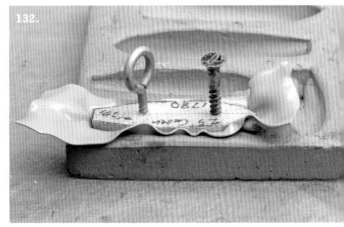

132.

When the plastic has softened sufficiently the mould is withdrawn from under the grill and the male mould pressed firmly in place and held there for a few seconds while the plastic hardens.

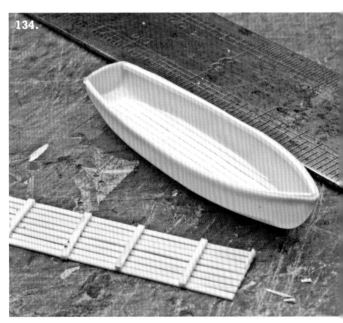

134.

One of *Caesar*'s motor boats; a strip of plastic has been fitted inside the gunwale and floorboards prepared as shown in the foreground fitted to the inside of the hull.

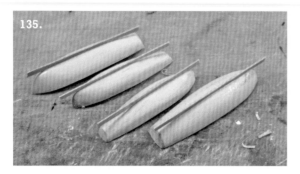

135.
Strips of boxwood have been cut to size for the keels and they have been glued to the hulls.

136.
Stems have been cut and fitted and at the stern wedges of wood inserted between the hull and the keel. As can be seen they are considerably wider than the keel to allow for blending them in to the hull.

137.
Now to return to *Caesar's* boats. As can be seen here I have on this occasion used polystyrene rather than boxwood for the keel and stem and am now in the process of planking the hull. This was done with paper planks glued in place with Seccotine. Plastic and Seccotine definitely do not work well together but it is an ideal glue to use when readjustments may be needed. To counter this problem the whole of the planked areas were given a coat of the ever-useful thin Superglue after the planking was completed, ensuring a very strong structure indeed. This is a technique that does require some practice, but it is well worth mastering. In practice the glue is flooded on fairly liberally and any residue wiped away *immediately* with a lint-free cloth or tissue in one swift pass or the cloth will be permanently glued to the hull, as the very thin Superglues have virtually instant grab.

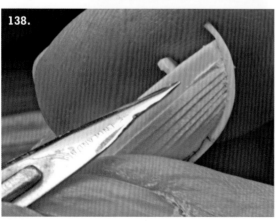

138.
At the bow the planks butt up against one another, only starting to overlap a short distance aft. To facilitate this, after each plank is laid, a wedge-shaped section was cut away as shown.

139.
The interiors of the boats taking shape. The whaler has three fine brass etched gratings, timbers and a keelbox. All have a rising to support the thwarts; these were cut from boxwood before being lightly stained with a little artists' oil colour mixed with polyurethane varnish. The thwart knees were cut to a triangular shape, the final profile being introduced after fitting using a diamond burr. A dodger made from tissue applied over a wire frame has been fitted to the 16ft fast motor dinghy and in the foreground are the cabin sides for the 25ft fast motor cutters.

139.

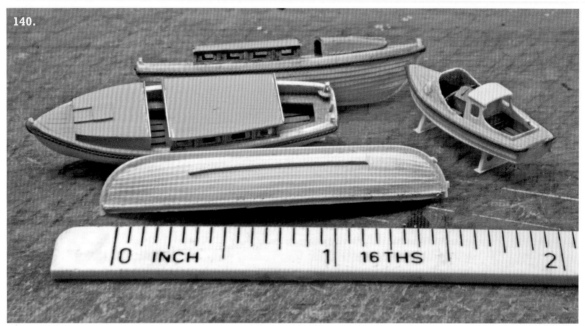

140.

140.
The boats nearing completion. Those areas made from plastic card that will be finished as varnished or natural wood have been painted with a pale buff undercoat. Where a varnished finish will be required they are subsequently given several coats of the stain used for the thwarts. The rope rubbing strake is made from lengths of copper wire wound together in a drill chuck.

141.
Oars are needed for the whaler and also for the Carley floats; these were made from brass wire, the blades being formed by hammering the ends flat on the steel block. They were then mounted one at a time in a pin vice and the ends of the shafts thinned with a diamond burr while continuously rotating the pin vice between the fingers.

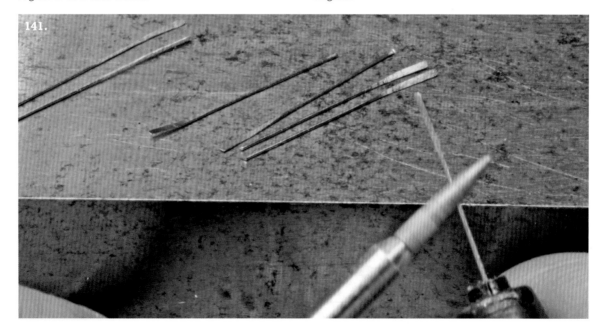

141.

142.

When, many years ago now, I made up my sheets of brass etch components, I included some davits suitable for a destroyer, so I made use of them here. Without them I would have used copper or brass wire beaten flat after shaping. Paper strips were glued to them to form the H section bar they were made from.

144.

The whaler in its davits giving a good view of the H section davits, the brass oars having been painted and stained. The rudder stored beneath the thwarts and grab ropes formed from semicircles of painted wire fitted beneath the rubbing strake.

143.

The starboard 25ft motor cutter fitted to the model. The falls and indeed all the rigging on the model are made from pre-painted copper wire, the blocks being made from punched disks of card. The webbing gripping bands were made from paper glued to a length of the same wire. The windows were glazed with 'Kristal Clear'. Much used by aircraft modellers, this is a glue-like compound applied to the opening with a pin, which is perfectly transparent when it dries, ideal for applications like this. Note also the brass handles fitted to the cabin trunks which allowed the latter to be removed by the crew.

145.
There are a number of cork floats attached around the superstructure. These were very easy to manufacture from polystyrene as shown here.

146.
The detailing was slightly more complicated to decipher. I eventually worked out that there were grab ropes fitted as shown here at various stages of the work . . .

147.
. . . and retaining ropes like these to tie them to the superstructure.

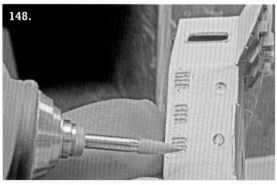

148.
As these were pre-painted surfaces, I roughed up the areas where they were to be fitted using a diamond burr, before gluing them in place with a blob of some fairly thick Superglue.

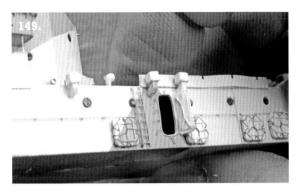

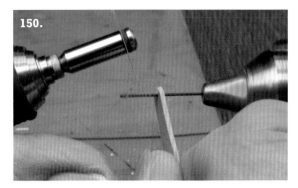

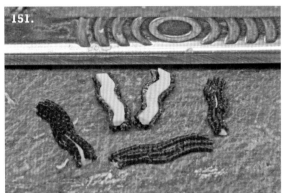

149.
Four of the floats fitted to the forward superstructure.

150.
Now to move on to the float nets, quite a noticeable feature in many of the photographs. I experimented with various methods of constructing these rather tricky items before settling on this one. First of all I prepared some plastic rod as demonstrated here; a length was chucked in the Minicraft drill and supported with the boxwood crutch and then just touched with the circular saw blade at regular intervals. Not quite as easy as it might appear, but if you cut too far it really doesn't matter, short sections will be just as useful as longer ones.

151.
Basic formers for the nets are then cut from some thick plastic card, rounded on one side and the nets assembled as shown.

152.
I have made no mention of the Carley floats. These were made from electrical wire of the correct size; the sort with a single heavy copper wire running through it. Correct lengths, using trial and error, were cut off and the wire poked through about 1/8in or so, each then shaped to the correct oval and the protruding end of the wire Superglued into the other end. After final adjusting for shape the grab ropes of fine thread were fitted followed by the brass etched centre (the centres can be just as easily manufactured from plastic or wood). The photograph shows two of the float nets and two Carley floats on the finished model.

▪ Depth Charges, Searchlights and Ventilators ▪

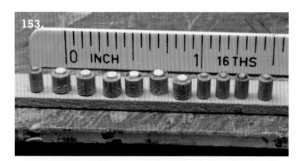

153.
A selection of depth charges and smoke floats, cut to size from boxwood dowel. The primer covers are punched from card.

154.
The launching rails on the stern. I made up some angle section from paper; this is quite simple to do by folding the paper before cutting close to the fold with a knife and steel ruler, and then opening it up to a 90-degree angle. The deck was then drilled to take the uprights, the deck being made good around them with dabs of Superglue applied with a fine wire. Then the lower rails were fitted followed by the depth charges, and the remainder of the structure was then built over them.

155.
The depth-charge racks under construction. I thought these were going to be quite straightforward, but constructing a rack to hold half-a-dozen depth charges proved near-impossible if a symmetrical finish was to be hoped for. I eventually settled on making three platforms from very dark grey card for each of the racks and mounting two depth charges on each. These were then glued one on top of another to provide a solid and square structure on which to fit the framework.

156.
After the framework of the rack has been completed, the legs are trimmed to length to accommodate the camber of the deck. Next, holes were drilled in the bottom platform and wires glued in place; these will be inserted and glued in holes drilled in the deck.

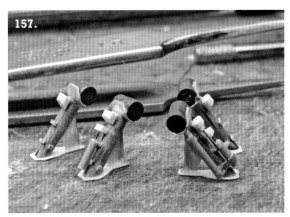

157.
The depth-charge throwers were really quite straightforward to construct, certainly less of a headache than the racks. The photograph should be self-explanatory; they are being made from a mix of wood, paper, plastic and wire.

159.
The stern of the model showing rails and stowage for three depth charges each side.

158.
Racks and throwers being fitted to the decks. The need for legs of differing lengths on the racks can clearly be seen. Rather than fit a dowel or pin to the base of the throwers, they have been glued directly to the deck and then a hole drilled down through the thrower into the deck, then, as shown here, a wire pin was dipped in glue and inserted; the remainder was then snipped off and tidied up with a diamond burr. For ease of access it is worth noting that I am doing this work before fitting the aft superstructure.

160.
The completed throwers, racks and also three of the smoke floats fitted on the starboard side. These last two photographs also show the draught marks. I always like to paint these on a model using a very fine sable brush. It is possible I believe to use transfers or Letraset but if you can manage to do it by hand I feel it looks rather less clinical.

161.
There are three searchlights required for *Caesar*, a 44in one mounted just aft of the funnel and two 20in ones on the bridge wings. Rather than make a hollow shell for them and fit a punched acetate disk as I have done in the past, I decided to build them from some solid polystyrene rod. This was 'turned' to the correct diameter using sanding boards. The end was given a domed finish for the rear of the lights and after parting them off they were re-chucked to finish the front 'glass end' flat. This end was then finished to a high gloss with 1000 grit 'wet-and-dry' followed by metal polish.

162.

Paper shells were then fitted to the outside, and the rear of the light given a couple of coats of white paint.

162.

163.

The support for the 44in searchlight was turned from boxwood as was the supporting column that will be fitted beneath the platform; box was also used for the cradle, which was sawn, filed and drilled to shape. When turning the support a peg was left below to fit the column and another was left on the top to fit a hole drilled in the cradle.

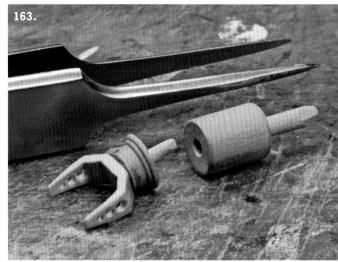

163.

164.

The circular platform was punched from card; the uprights were then glued to the underside and folded upwards at the correct angle. The railings were formed by winding the wire round a variety of punches and drill bits. They were glued in place with Superglue.

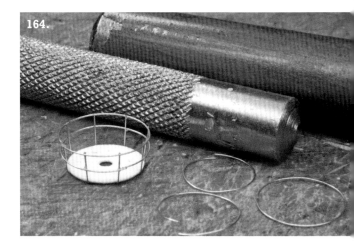

164.

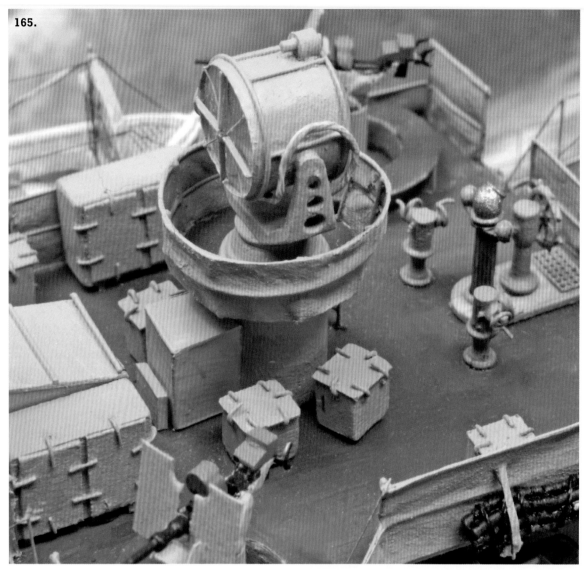

165.

165.
The completed searchlight after being detailed. The rims around the light are copper wire as is the cable. The canvas dodgers are tissue-paper fitted while damp. The photo also gives good close-up views of the emergency steering position and the single Oerlikons and float nets, or parts of them at least.

166.
There are many ventilators to be made on any warship model. Here is a selection. On this model I have used plastic card, rod and tube. They should be made long enough to be inserted directly into holes drilled in the deck rather than be glued directly to it.

166.

167.

Several small cowl ventilators are also required. I made the cowl by chucking some boxwood dowel, hollowing the inside as shown here with a diamond burr before finishing as much as reasonably possible of the outside with the same burr and then parting off. The shaft was then shaped to fit the cowl and the two sections glued together, the Superglue filling the join, they were finally cleaned up and painted.

168.

I made the lumber and cordage racks by winding wire over a wooden frame as described later in the book (see photograph 178). They were formed in one piece as shown in the foreground before being folded to shape.

169.

Quite a few cordage reels were needed throughout the ship, and they are very simple to make. These small ones are lengths of dowel with punched paper ends, which have been drilled to accept the wire for the handles. The wire legs made long enough to fit into holes drilled in the deck. They were finally wound with some pre-painted wire cordage. There are larger and slightly more complicated ones just forward of 'A' gun but they are basically the same design any extra framework added using paper or card. The tweezers have been fitted with thin strips of card to prevent the painted cordage from being damaged while working on them

170.

170.
The lumber rack fitted beside the funnel: the cordage rack has been fitted on the opposite side. I fixed these in place by fitting a couple of wire pins down through the timber and into the deck before gluing the final layers of timber and rope on top. It is not always possible to pin or dowel very small details but I like to whenever I can. Just aft of them are the beef screen and potato locker; they are made from some very fine zinc grating and

then detailed with paper, pins were fitted to the legs in same manner as they were to the depth-charge racks. Two of the cordage reels can be seen in the foreground.

171.
This view of the bow of the ship takes in the reels mentioned in photograph 169 as well as the ground tackle. The anchors were constructed from boxwood and paper.

171.

▪ The Sea ▪

172.

For many years now I have carved my seas from timber, and consider it to be, for me anyway, the best and most expressive material from which to make them. Should you choose this method experiment with various timbers and get a feel for the technique before tackling an actual sea.

Before starting to carve the waves a recess needs to be cut to accept the model, and some time should be spent making the decision about exactly where you want it to sit. I initially routed this recess making it slightly smaller than the waterline dimensions of the model to allow for final trimming to size. This was done by repeatedly offering the hull up to the sea, marking in, and then carefully trimming the edge back little by little with either chisels and gouges, or a suitable burr in the Minicraft drill. If the ship is to be heeling to port or starboard then the recess will either have to be cut deeper on one side or, if the recess is of sufficient depth, a small batten of wood can be glued to one side. There is quite a lot of trial and error getting the ship to sit 'just right' in the board and it is quite

important to continually try and visualise the ship in the finished sea while the carving progresses. Before making a start the wave crests should be marked in and while carving always keep in mind the wind direction and the appearance of the final picture you wish to create.

I usually carve the sea with a variety of gouges. When attempting to carve a sea from wood there are two essential requirements, the right timber and razor-sharp tools, but it is not always easy finding suitable timber for this purpose. As I mentioned I have in the past used lime very successfully but my supply of seasoned timber no longer included any of sufficient length for *Caesar*'s sea. I eventually sourced a rather expensive, well-seasoned piece of bass wood that looked perfect for the job, but when I reached the carving stage I found it was rather brittle and prone to tearing even when using the sharpest of tools, as you may be able to see in the accompanying photograph. Rather than start a new hunt for suitable timber at this late stage I decided to carve the sea with carbide cutters.

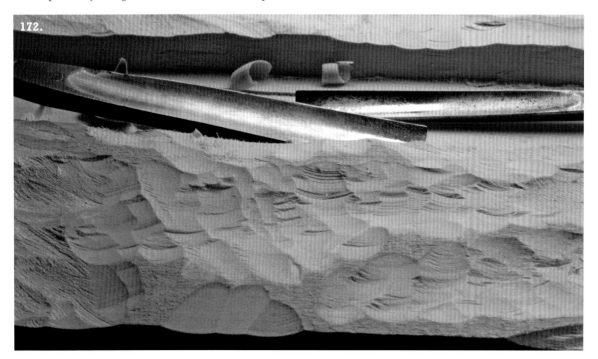

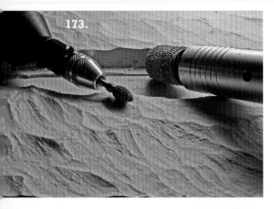

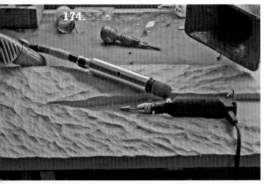

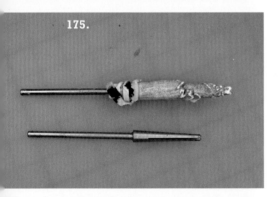

173.

Carving with these carbide bitts is not something we come across very often, particularly in this country, but they are widely used in the US for wildlife and especially decoy carving. I came across them when making a brief foray into this field many years ago. One of the skills I learned and brought back to my ship modelling was the use of these cutters, not just for seas as demonstrated here but for many other tasks. I would be rather lost nowadays without my rotary tools as perusal of these pages will confirm. For any ship modellers wishing to explore the uses and quite amazing results achieved with these tools try Googling 'decoy carving'.

Now back to the task in hand. The main troughs and crests were introduced with the 1in-diameter bit on the right of the picture, here being used in a flexible-shaft tool; this will literally breeze through most woods but as you can see it leaves a very rough finish. This can be reduced to some extent by working over and further refining the waves with the finer bit in the Minicraft tool on the left.

174.

The final cutter to be used is the ruby; this gives quite a fine finish while still having enough cutting power for the job. Only the left-hand side of the sea has been worked on so far.

175.

For a really good finish some form of sanding or wire-wooling is required. Doing this by hand it is all too easy to lose the definition introduced with the carvers. One answer is to use a split mandrel as shown in this photograph. Use some very fine grit paper and work over the sea as you would with a carver, working into the troughs rather than across their crests.

If you do not have, or cannot obtain, one of these mandrels a serviceable home-made version can be easily made from a nail, using a junior hacksaw to cut the slot. To prepare for use, a strip of sandpaper is inserted in the slot before winding it round the mandrel, finally holding it in place with an elastic band.

176.

Some form of permanent fixing should be organised at this stage to ensure the model is fitted in exactly its final position before dealing with the bow wave and any filling required around the hull. With the model firmly in place I drilled down through the hull beneath both the forward and aft superstructure positions to produce a hole a tight fit for a bolt. The hull was removed and the bolts screwed tightly into the now rebated holes which were then flooded with Superglue. The holes in the sea were then enlarged slightly and rebated underneath to allow for the fitting of washers and nuts.

177.

The final job in the shaping of the sea is to add bow wave, wake and wave crests. The hull was wrapped in Clingfilm, taking care to get as smooth a finish as possible around the waterline. Next I prepared some Milliput epoxy putty and rolled out some thin strips, which were pressed firmly in place around the top of the inside of the recess for the hull. These strips were then treated to a good warm-up with a hair dryer to soften the putty and then the model was pressed firmly into the recess and the washers and nuts fitted and tightened until the model was sitting at the correct water level both fore and aft. Finally, using a modelling tool or a sharpened strip of boxwood, trim away the putty that will have oozed up the side of the hull and shape, from some fresh putty, the bow wave, wave crests etc. When dry trim back the Clingfilm so that the model can be removed before peeling away the remains of the Clingfilm. Sometimes models can be quite

stubborn to remove, but a few gentle taps on the ends of the screwed rods usually does the trick. The sea can now be given several coats of undercoat. I prefer something quite neutral like a mid grey – white can take several coats of enamel to completely kill it. In between coats a gentle rubdown with fine wire wool should be given. I paint my seas with Humbrol Enamels, and spend quite a time mixing the exact colours and shades that I think I shall need. Then I just wade in, the darker shades go on first, even darker close to the hull, then before it can dry, lighter areas are blended in towards the tops of the waves, finally the crests are painted white. When dry it can be given a couple of coats of varnish. I personally do not think that it is a good idea to automatically use gloss: it is OK for a glassy calm but where the wind whips across the waves and the tiny ripples produce a matting effect, then a satin finish would seem appropriate.

177.

▪ Final Assembly ▪

178.

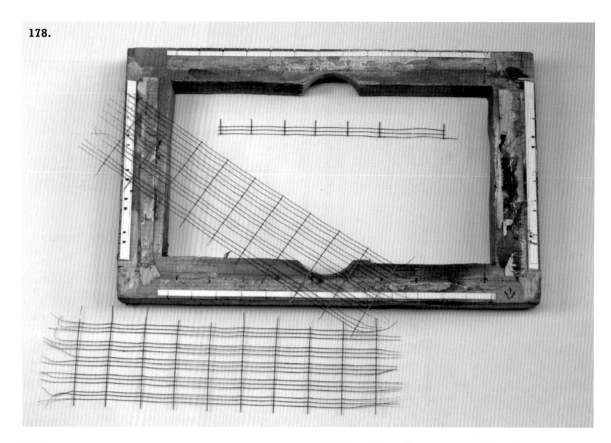

178.

The railings for the main and forecastle decks were formed on a simple wooden jig. This is a technique I have mentioned elsewhere in this volume for other applications and, using a slightly different jigs, have used them for many years for forming shroud and ratline assemblies for sailing vessels. It is a method well worth perfecting, all it involves to produce very lifelike railings for a variety of miniature scales, is care and patience.

The jig can be cut from any rigid timber or fibreboard; I have a variety of them for different uses. This one is made from a piece of 6in x 4in x 1/2in plywood. At top and bottom a strip of thin card has been glued and marked with positions for the stanchions, at either side are strips of thick card marked out for the wire railings, and identically-marked strips of card are applied to the other side of the jig in exactly corresponding positions. Now the

winding of the railings can start; first of all the wire railings are wound around the jig, three for each of the railings, taking great care to position them exactly the same distance apart and doing so on both sides of the jig. When this is completed and the end tied or glued off, the stanchions are wound using a slightly thicker wire. Because they are wound over the thinner card they will pull down onto the rails, ensuring a good contact. Now, using a piece of wire, Superglue is run down the length of each of the stanchion wires and when the joins are checked and OK, the railings can be cut free from the jig. Before performing this final task I like to run a needle or some other smooth tool along each of the rails to induce a slight dip to each. This is only occasionally observable in photographs, the wires normally being set very tight, but I think it adds a little life and movement, and gives the feel of a slightly sagging wire railing rather than a rigid steel one.

179.

The rigid steel railings on the ship were built up individually as shown here, many of them being subsequently covered with 'tissue-paper' canvas dodgers. Also seen clearly in this picture are some of the ammunition lockers to found throughout the ship. They were made from boxwood, cut to size on the Preac saw, before fitting with card lids or doors and wire clips.

180.

Another photograph taken at the assembly stage showing a feature not touched on so far, one of the gangways between the superstructure decks. They were very simply made from Bristol board with paper sides, all well impregnated with the ever-useful thin Superglue, and they are straightforward to fit. I always felt they were a most attractive feature on these later destroyers, adding interest and visually making a link with and drawing together the different decks. Also of note here are the handrails around the outside of the superstructure; individual wire pins were fitted for the ends of each section, which were then trimmed off short and the rails glued to them. The final item to go on the model is the rigging, nothing very complex here; it was all done with pre-painted wire and Superglue, the insulators being formed from blobs of white glue.

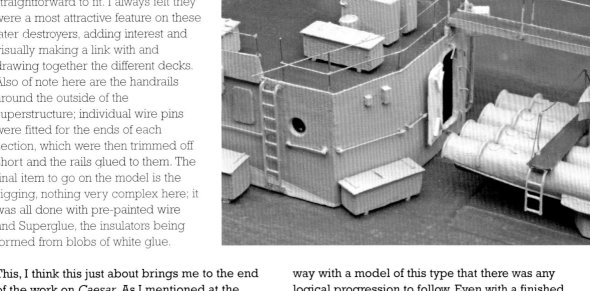

This, I think this just about brings me to the end of the work on *Caesar*. As I mentioned at the beginning of the book it would not slavishly follow my journey through the model. Had it done so it would have been horribly disjointed with all the chopping and changing of direction that went on. Sometimes items were put in the drawer half-finished awaiting more research information but even with the order the parts of the ship and the fittings were made there was no way with a model of this type that there was any logical progression to follow. Even with a finished hull, superstructure and fittings to hand I suspect no two modelmakers would follow the same sequence of assembly. With *Caesar* I followed the basic principle of fitting out a miniature model: the least vulnerable first, and as far as possible working from the centreline outwards. One of the joys of this work is that there are no rules: you make them up as you go along.

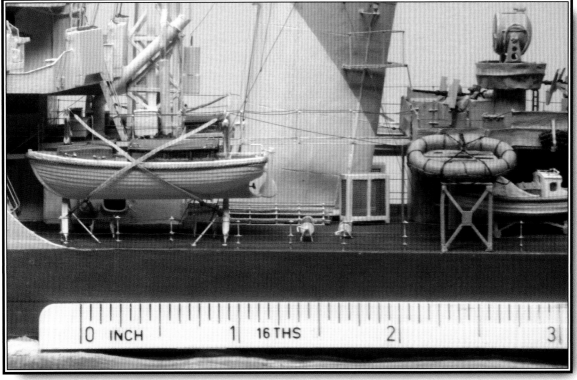

▪ Model Gallery ▪

HMS *Belfast* and HMS *Bluebell* Scale 50ft to 1in

HMS *Belfast* was a Modified 'Town' class cruiser, one of the two final ships of the 'Town' class. She was completed soon after the outbreak of the Second World War but was badly damaged by a German mine early in her service, only returning to active duty in late 1942. She saw action escorting convoys in the Atlantic and Arctic and participated in the battle of North Cape. In 1944 she supported the D-Day landings and saw further action during the Korean War. She is now preserved as a museum ship in the Port of London.

HMS *Bluebell* was one of the 'Flower' class corvettes that featured so prominently in the Battle of the Atlantic. She first entered service in 1940 and was torpedoed and sunk while escorting a Russian convoy from Murmansk in February 1941

These two models provide something of a seminal point in my modelmaking career, marking a transition I made from plastic kits to purely scratch-built models, and as such may give hope and direction to those amongst you who find the idea of scratch-building overly daunting. After the *Curacao* project was shelved (see Introduction) it was some time before I returned to the idea of a modern warship model. Quite what the sequence of events was some thirty-seven years ago I can no longer recall but having at hand a copy of *Flower Class Corvettes* in the Ensign series and an Airfix plastic kit of HMS *Belfast*, I decided on the diorama you see here.

Examination of the kit parts showed much that would, I felt, be totally unacceptable in a properly-finished model particularly when displayed alongside what would be, I hoped, the more delicate and in scale model of *Bluebell*. You must remember here that I was comparatively new to modelmaking, totally new to modern warships and these model kits, back then, were largely sold to youngsters. I had not heard of the methods of detailing and improving them that are mainstream nowadays and, as far as I am aware, there were no extra fittings or photo-etched parts available that are such a feature of the model kit world today, and, can you believe it, I had never even <u>heard</u> of plastic card!

So to bring the kit to an acceptable (to me) level meant making a few radical changes using the materials I had at hand: wood, paper and wire. The models I so much admired all had 'real' wood decks so I decided my *Belfast* would as well, so the planked decks were all cut away and a fairly hefty pre-shaped sycamore deck inserted. In order to bring these right to the edge I seem to remember chamfering the inside of the hull along its top edge and chamfering the edges of the deck. Before they were fitted they were all marked with scale width planks drawn in with a very hard and sharp pencil. Amongst the other modifications were the removal of all the oversize bulwarks and splinter plating and their replacement with paper ones and the remodelling of the Walrus seaplane, rigging it with fine wire. New cranes were constructed from copper wire purloined from electrical wire; railings, various aerials, 20mm gun barrels, funnel cage, masts and spars and rigging were all once again manufactured from scraps of wire from the same source and the boats were hollowed out before being detailed with wood shavings and paper. Some of this work I can still remember, some thirty-five years later, as clearly as if it were yesterday, but much else has to be deduced from the photographs. The work on *Bluebell* is, I'm afraid, equally hazy. I can remember the hull and superstructure being carved from a very fine-grained hardwood, probably holly or sycamore, as would have been the superstructures, with detailing of paper and wire. What I do remember clearly is the frustration and difficulties I experienced working at such a small scale for the first time.

HMS *Cossack* Scale 16ft to 1in

HMS *Cossack* was a 'Tribal' class destroyer completed in June 1938. Her first and most famous action was in February 1946 when she freed the *Admiral Graf Spee*'s prisoners who were being held aboard the supply ship *Altmark*. In April of the same year she took part in the Second Battle of Narvik and In May 1941 participated in the pursuit and sinking of the *Bismarck*. In October of the same year, while escorting a convoy from Gibraltar to the UK, she was sunk by a torpedo from *U-563*.

Having finished the previous model I had an unaccountable feeling of lack of satisfaction with the result and I am sure that this was nothing to do with its final appearance but rather because I had based it on a kit, and I felt that the work was not really mine. I should say here that I trained exclusively in Fine Art, virtually from the age of thirteen until twenty-one, so had many years of being conditioned to starting with a blank page or canvas, the work obviously having to be all my own from the ground up, so to speak. So I suppose it was a degree of guilt or conditioning.

There were a great many models on display in museums that had obviously been produced with speed in mind with a decidedly crude finish and lack of fine detail, in order, I imagine, to illustrate the many and varied ships in service during the first half of the twentieth century and not cost the earth to commission. These were the ones I was drawn to at this time, basing a model on one of these seemed a possibility, something within my capabilities, unlike the complex and detailed builders' models and even more so those incredible models by Norman Ough.

I had by this time planned to build a model of *Cossack*, already having acquired a set of plans but I needed visual explanations and back-up for these. I knew from a previous visit to the Imperial War Museum that they had a model of a 'Tribal', so when driving home to Cornwall from a visit to my parents who lived in Essex I managed to make a very brief visit to the Museum. I managed to park my Morris 1000 van right outside and armed with a very basic camera, and a copy of *The 'Tribals'* by Martin H Brice, on the flyleaf of which I had listed twenty-two questions for which I needed answers, scooted in to the museum under a considerable degree of stress, as I had left a wife, a Siamese cat

and a parrot waiting in the van – a potentially volatile mix – I had to work fast. I have that copy of *The 'Tribals'* in front of me at this moment, the inside of both covers, flyleaf and title page are all covered with notes and annotated drawings, none of them works of art, but they meant at long last I had the necessary material for a scratch-built model.

I can remember little of the building of *Cossack*. It would have been built from wood, paper and wire; it has remained in the possession of my sister, so I managed to take the photographs that you see here. It is rather basic to say the least, but it was a first, and the excitement I experienced building it, the overcoming each new problem and the sense of achievement on its completion, were very real. It makes you realise that it is not just the standard or quality of a model that is the measure of its success but the personal satisfaction and growth that they bring to their creator.

HMS *Hood* Scale 32ft to 1in

During the inter-war years the battlecruiser HMS *Hood* was celebrated as the pride of the Royal Navy. She was also generally accepted as being one of the most perfectly proportioned and impressive warships of her day – something I would heartily agree with – her balanced profile exhibited an impression of both power and speed. Her tragic end came when she was sunk by the German battleship *Bismarck* on 24 May 1941.

After completing the previous model I must have had a surge of confidence, moving on so peremptorily from a destroyer to a battlecruiser, I remember photographing in detail a fine model of *Hood* at the Imperial War Museum. I also had copies of the Ensign special *'HOOD Design and Construction'* by Maurice Northcott and Profile No. 19, both of which had good photographs, including on-board ones, of her in 1920, one of the reasons I chose to depict her at this date. The ensign publication also had general arrangement plans for the ship for 1920, so there were no major research problems. I had also obtained a copy of Norman Ough's plans; these helped with some of the details and fittings but they should, like all plans actually, be checked in every way possible for inaccuracies. There is one other important reference, and one I would recommend to anyone

tackling this ship with its forward superstructure built around the tripod mast for the first time, and that is the drawing by John Bowen in *Model Shipwright* No. 1. He gives a very clear breakdown for this feature, admittedly for the scale of 50ft to 1in, but the only real difference at this larger scale is the amount of detail that can be added.

I had very recently discovered plastic card and for a number of years, apart from the hull, which I carved from timber, used this material almost exclusively for my small-scale warships. It has the great advantage of coming in a multitude of thicknesses and being very easy to work with the most basic of tools, very suitable for my circumstances at this time when I was doing most of my modelmaking on a wooden tray at the living-room table. There were one or two exceptions; the massive tripod mast was made from brass tubing, brass rod was used to turn the funnels for the pinnaces and wire used for rigging and railings. A point of interest is the 'wooden' decks: for the first and I think only time I did not use a natural wood finish for them, but instead painted them a natural wood colour, followed by a coat of matt polyurethane varnish. This was then very finely rubbed down with wire wool before lining the decks with a 0.1 Rapidograph.

HMS *Penelope* Scale 32ft to 1in

HMS *Penelope* was an *Arethusa* class cruiser, completed in 1936. She had an eventful war service extending from Norway to the Mediterranean. She was damaged many times, on one occasion earning the name 'Pepper Pot' from extensive shrapnel damage. She was finally sunk by a torpedo from *U-410* in February 1944. The novel *The Ship* by C S Forester is modelled on *Penelope*'s part in the First Battle of the Sirte. Recommended reading for any warship aficionado.

The techniques used for this model were virtually identical to those for the previous one, the one noticeable difference being the decks, these were the natural timber used for the hull and superstructures, they were also given a coat or two of polyurethane to seal them before being given the same treatment as the *Hood*'s. You may note that at this time and for some years to come my seas are not carved from wood but built up with Polyfilla.

HMS *Lapwing* Scale 32ft to 1in

HMS *Lapwing* was one of the Modified *Black Swan* class of frigates that played such a prominent part in convoy protection and anti-submarine warfare during the latter half of the Second World War. She had a tragically short career, being torpedoed off Northern Russia just a year after being first commissioned.

This little model was also built predominantly from plastic card, and as originally completed was presented in a calm sea as shown in the black-and-white photograph. When completed it went to a London gallery for sale; it had not been on display for long before it was stolen and I assumed that would be the last I would hear of her. But then several years later she turned up at auction in the US and was bought by a East Coast gallery, in, I believe, a damaged state. They contacted me to see if indeed it was my model and asked if I could make any necessary repairs, add some weathering and remount her in a more dramatic sea, a request I dutifully complied with, as can be seen in the colour pictures.

HMS *Black Prince* Scale 32ft to 1ft

Black Prince was a Modified *Dido* class cruiser, first entering service in late 1943, serving initially on convoy protection duties in the Arctic; she supported the Normandy landings and later served in the Far East and Pacific. In May 1946 she was transferred to the Royal New Zealand Navy.

I think the *Dido* class were particularly well-balanced and attractive ships with the added bonus of being well covered in *Ensign No. 2* which also gives a whole variety of camouflage schemes for the class, always a bonus. The techniques used were still timber hull and superstructures, covered and detailed with plastic card.

HMS *King George V* Scale 32ft to 1in

HMS *King George V* was first commissioned during
December 1940 and was initially involved with
convoy duties before transferring to the
Mediterranean to cover the Sicily landings. From
1944 until Japan surrendered she served with the
British Pacific Fleet, being present off Japan during
the surrender ceremony. In 1946 she was re-
commissioned as flagship of the Home Fleet until
being decommissioned and scrapped in 1957.
The one thing that sticks in my memory about this
model was the amount of repetitive work that it
involved. It was a commissioned model so had to
be finished within a set period. I was still teaching
at that time and also moving house, making it
rather more of an endurance test than a pleasure,
which was a shame, but you can't win them all. She
was the final predominantly plastic-card model in
the series of small-scale warships that I built.

HMS *Onslow* Scale 16ft to 1in

HMS *Onslow* was another war-built destroyer made famous as one of the group who defended a Russian convoy against the German pocket battleship *Lützow* and heavy cruiser *Admiral Hipper*. If you are looking for a thundering good read try *73 NORTH: The Battle of the Barents Sea* by Dudley Pope. This gives a full account of this event, it's as gripping as any novel.

I chose her as a subject because of the excellent photographs and drawings in the *Ensign No. 6* publication which I already possessed, and also as a set of plans were printed by A&A plans. However, it turned out these were unavailable at the time for some reason or another so I ordered a set from the National Maritime Museum, who provided a fast, efficient and affordable service in those far-off halcyon days.

The basic principals outlined for *Caesar* would apply reasonably well to this model, which, as I remember now had the hull carved from a block of pine with most of the remaining work being carried out with plastic card.

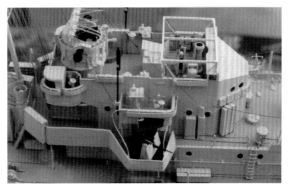

HMS *Dorsetshire* Scale 32ft to 1in

After first commissioning in 1930 HMS *Dorsetshire* became the flagship of the 2nd Cruiser Squadron and thereafter served in the Atlantic and on the Africa and China Stations until 1939. At the outbreak of war she operated in the Atlantic for a short time before monitoring French forces off Dakar throughout July 1940. In May 1941 *Dorsetshire* took part in the pursuit of the *Bismarck*, finally delivering the torpedoes that rang her death knell. In 1942 she was transferred to the Eastern Fleet where on 5 April she was sunk by Japanese bombers.

I have very fond memories of building this model. I had had a couple of years virtually devoid of modelmaking in order to set up and try and run my own pottery. As I was still teaching this had to be fitted in evenings, weekends and holidays, leaving little time to spare for the ships. But I was pining for them even as the pottery with its commitments took off. I eventually accepted the inevitable, closed down the business, sold the equipment and converted the rather ramshackle shed I had built into my first purpose-built model workshop. *Dorsetshire* was the first model to emerge from it. She was built in much the same manner as the earlier ones though with more reliance on traditional materials such as paper and card. I was also by this time planking all the wood decks with individual planks cut from wood shavings mounted on tissue-paper; something of a step forward from the lined decks of the early models.

HMS *Iron Duke* Scale 32ft to 1in

HMS *Iron Duke* was first commissioned in 1914 and served as flagship of the Grand Fleet during the First World War, her only major engagement being at the battle of Jutland. After the war she served as a base ship at Scapa Flow. She was finally scrapped in 1948.

Several years had gone by since I completed *Dorsetshire* and I had been experimenting with new techniques while working on miniature sailing vessels, on starting this model I made use of many of them to see how they worked on a warship. All the superstructures were from timber, decks fitted to the tripod mast were cut from Bristol board and the wood decks were all individually planked. The accompanying drawings were made at the time of the model's construction and give a detailed breakdown of the materials used when modelling the tripod mast. Having been using tissue-paper for making sails I used the same techniques for the quarterdeck awning and the sails for the launch.

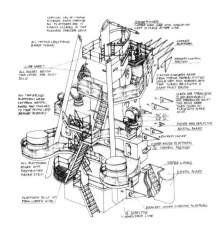

HMS *Edinburgh* Scale 32ft to 1in

HMS *Edinburgh* was a Modified 'Town' class cruiser, one of only two that were built, the sister-ship to HMS *Belfast*. First commissioned in July 1939 she served most of her life on convoy or patrol duty whilst serving with the Home Fleet, finally being torpedoed in the Barents Sea in May 1942. At the time of her sinking she was carrying 465 gold ingots packed in ninety-three wooden boxes. After the war the British Government were understandably interested in salvaging the gold and in 1954 the salvage rights were offered to a UK company but the project was put on hold due to the strained relations between the West and the Soviet Union. Late in the 1970s the Government was once again showing interest in retrieving the gold before it could be either pirated or claimed by the Soviets, so contracted 'Jessop Marine' to undertake the salvage. Work proceeded

smoothly until bad weather forced an end to the diving operation, however by that time 431 of the 465 ingots had been recovered.

This model was commissioned by the Parker Gallery on behalf of the salvage company, and came with the request that she be shown exactly as she appeared at the time of her sinking. This proved to be almost impossible, many of the minor changes in her appearance being unrecorded and photographic evidence to say the least was sketchy and vague. After many letters were written and received usable plans were compiled but it proved impossible to establish the colour and pattern of her camouflage scheme so it was agreed that she be painted an overall 507B medium grey. The same basic methods and materials used for the previous model were used for *Edinburgh*.

HMS *Penelope* **Scale 16ft to 1in**

This is the second model of HMS *Penelope* shown here but as she is built to twice the scale, with different materials and many years after the earlier one I decided, in keeping with the other models, that she should remain where she sequentially belongs. This was a model I greatly enjoyed building. She is, like many British cruisers, handsome and well-balanced, with a wealth of varied detail throughout the ship. The detail work on the floatplane, catapult and crane were particularly involving and you may note the rather enthusiastic carving of the wooden sea, a technique I was fairly new to.

HMS *Dreadnought* Scale 32ft to 1in

HMS *Dreadnought* was of such a revolutionary design with her ten 12in guns in five twin turrets that she not only sparked off an international arms race but gave her name to a whole generation of battleships, the 'Dreadnoughts'. She entered service in 1907 and after extensive and very successful trials became flagship of the Home Fleet 1907–12. At the outbreak of First World War she became the flagship of the 4th Battle Squadron based at Scapa Flow, her only action of any significance was the ramming and sinking of a German U-boat. She went into reserve in 1919 and was scrapped in 1922.

This model and the following one of HMS *Canada* were a pair of models commissioned by the Parker Gallery on behalf of a South American client. They are at odds with the title of this book, being full-hull models. Not the presentation I personally would have chosen as I feel modern warships work far better as waterline subjects. One feature I had a problem with was the torpedo nets. Any actual netting being obviously out of the question at this scale, I eventually settled on some suitable string which when dyed with watercolour paint worked quite well. The plinths and cases for the models were made from solid figured oak (I believe this wood was requested by the client); I managed to obtain a plank of nicely seasoned timber and spent many hours cutting, shaping and sanding them to shape.

HMS *Canada* Scale 32ft to 1in

HMS *Canada* was originally ordered by the government of Chile as *Valparaiso* but being incomplete at the outbreak of the First World War was bought back by the British government and renamed *Canada*. She served with the Grand Fleet's 2nd Battle Squadron and took part in the battle of Jutland in 1916. Post-war she was refitted before being resold to Chile as the *Admirante Latorre*.

HMS *Dido* Scale 16ft to 1in

HMS *Dido* was the name ship of her class of light cruisers; she was commissioned in September 1940 serving initially with the Atlantic Fleet before being transferred to the Mediterranean, escorting convoys from Alexandria. She had an eventful war both in the Mediterranean and for a time in the Arctic, taking considerable damage and being repaired and refitted on several occasions. She survived the war and was held in reserve until being finally broken up in 1958.

I am sure you have noticed that the majority of the models so far have been built to the scale of 32ft to 1in. Most of them were commissions and the scale was part of my remit: a capital ship built to a larger scale than this can require quite a bit of house

room. *Dido* was a model that I had planned to build for some time with the intention of keeping her; the work was spread over two years from 1995–7 as I had other work that had to take precedence. I still think 16ft to 1in is the ideal scale to work to: it is possible to add a great deal of detail and the completed model is also capable of being appreciated and examined from a few feet away and becomes a real presence in a room. *Dido* is still with me. I built the case to fit an existing shelf in my bedroom where she is lit by a small spotlight when the bedside light is switched on. Most of the work was carried out using wood, paper and card with only a few isolated details being made from brass and plastic. She is shown at anchor in a calm sea and has a case of walnut veneer.

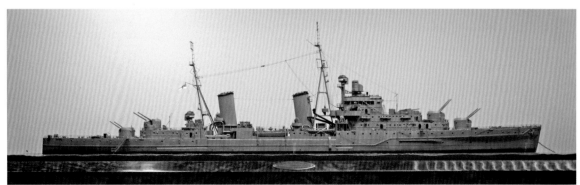

▪ Materials and Tools ▪

Below is a list of the suppliers of tools and materials, some of which have been mentioned in the text

IN THE UK

Douglas Electronic Industries Ltd, 55 Eastfield Road, Louth, Lincs LN11 7AL
Tel. 01507 603643
Can supply a suitable transformer for use in the UK with the Preac saw.

Maynard Ltd. Merretts Mill, Woodchester, Gloucestershire GL5 5EX
Tel. 01453 833185
Suppliers and repairers of Emco and Unimat lathes.

Squires Model and Craft Tools, 100 London Road, Bognor Regis, West Sussex PO21 1DD
Tel. 01243 842424
Fax 01243 842525
Suppliers of Minicraft tools, and many of the other model supplies that you are likely to need.

Axminster Tool Centre Ltd, Weycroft Avenue, Axminster, Devon EX13 5PH
Tel. 0800 371822
Fax 01297 35242
For a huge range of hand and power tools including Flex Cut chisels and gouges and some excellent sharpening materials including the 'TOMEK' range of grinding and sharpening tools.

Claudius Ash Sons and Co. Ltd., Summit House, Summit Road, Potters Bar, Hertfordshire EN6 3EE
Tel (Free Phone). 0800 090909
Fax 01707 649001
An excellent source of supply for the very fine diamond burrs that figure prominently in the photographs.

Swann-Morton Ltd., Owleton Green, Sheffield S6 2BJ
Tel. 0114 2344231
Fax 0114 231 4966
Suppliers of scalpels, knives and blades. I particularly like their SM-00 knife used with the SM01 blade.

General Woodwork Supplies (Stoke Newington) Ltd., 76-80 Stoke Newington High Street, London N16 7PA
Tel. 020 7254 6052
Fax 020 7254 7223
Suppliers of most timbers, which they will cut to your requirements

John Boddy Timber Ltd., Riverside Sawmills, Boroughbridge, North Yorkshire Y051 9LJ
Tel. 01423 322370
Fax 01423 323810
A good general timber supplier, for many timbers including jelutong.

Timberline, Unit 7, Munday Works, 58-66 Morley Road, Tonbridge, Kent TN9 1RP
Tel. 01732 355626
Fax (01732) 358214
Timbers including lemonwood.

Ormiston Wire Ltd., 1 Fleming Way, Worton Road, Isleworth, Middlesex TW7 6EU
Tel. 020 8569 7287
Fax 020 8569 8601
E-mail: info@ormiston-wire.ac.uk
Suppliers of most types of wire including the tinned copper that I have made extensive use of on this model.

The Airbrush & Spray Centre Ltd., 39 Littlehampton Road, Worthing, West Sussex BN13 1QJ
Tel. 08700 660445. E-mail: airbrush@lineone.net
All your airbrush needs.

Falkiners, 76, Southampton Row, London WC1B 4AR
Tel. 020 7831 1151
For supplies of Seccotine.

IN THE US

Preac Tool Co. Inc, 1596 Pea Pond Road, North Bellmore, New York USA NY 11710
Tel. 001-516-333-1500
Fax 5116-333-1501
E-mail: preac@crols.com
For the excellent miniature precision table saw, thicknesser etc.

Micro-Mark, 340-2656 Snyder Avenue, Berkely Heights NJ 07922
Good supplier of a great variety of tools.

Warner Woods West, P.O. Box 100, Irvins UT 84738
For wood supplies.

Lumber Yard, 6908 Stadium Drive, Brecksville OH 44141
Has a wide range of woods.

The following are good suppliers of general modelling materials.

K&S Engineering, 6917 W. 59th Street, Chicago IL 60638

Small Parts Inc, 13980 NW 58th Court, Miami Lakes FL 33014-0650

Ace Surgical Supply Co Inc, 1034 Pearl Street, Brockton MA 02301

Pelican Wire Co Inc, White Lake Corporate Park, 3650 Shaw Blvd. Naples, Florida 34117
Tel. 239 597 8555. Fax 239 597 9783

▪ Sources & Bibliography ▪

The plans used came from John Lambert Plans, available from the website: www.lambert-plans.com. Below is a list of books and periodicals which I have found useful sources of information during the construction of this and many other models. Though I am sure any warship aficionado who is also an aspiring modeller will have access to numerous others including the Internet, a resource still so new to me that I would not deign to offer advice on its navigation. Many of books are no longer in print and it may need diligent searching to locate copies.

Bowen, John (ed), *Scale Model Warships* (London 1978).
Good general reading and the section on armament is particularly useful.

Campbell, John, *Naval Weapons of World War Two* (London 1985; reprinted 2007).

Friedman, Norman, *British Destroyers and Frigates* (London 2006).

_____, *Naval Radar* (London 1981).

Goodman, Sydney, and Warlow, Ben, *The Royal Navy in Focus in World War 2 Part One*.
This series of paperbacks 9? x 7in each contain over 100 full-page photographs of individual ships. All are worth obtaining but I have singled out the above as it contains a good photograph of *Caesar*. They are published by Maritime Books, Liskeard, Cornwall. Worth checking out their website: www.navybooks.com

Hodges, Peter, and Friedman, Norman, *Destroyer Weapons of World 2* (London 1979).
Excellent reference, with many drawings and photographs.

Preston, Anthony, *Warship Profile No. 32 HMS* Cavalier *and the Ca Class Destroyers*.

Robertson, Stuart, and Dent, Stephen, *The War at Sea in Photographs 1939-1945* (London 2007).

Raven, Alan, and Roberts, John, *Ensign No 6 War Built Destroyers O-Z Classes* (1976).
All the Ensign series are well worth obtaining if you can, they all include plenty of on-board shots, drawings and camouflage information.

Williams, David, *Naval Camouflage 1914-1945* (London 2001).